Self Love Elevated

Compiled by Heather Andrews

Foreword by Christina Smith

Contributing Authors

Amber Louise
Jacqueline Lagrandeur
Melinda Pokolinski
Andrea Petrut
Jennifer Traynor
Reena Yost
Brittnie Hamilton
Jostine Bulan
Sarah Ommen
Catherine Huddleston
Kamilla Harra
Shannan Stella Roberts
Charlene Madden
Kara O'Daniel
Yassminne Atallah
Helena Smolok
Krista Enslow

Self Love Elevated

Print ISBN: 978-1-989848-29-6

Ebook ISBN: 978-1-989848-30-2

Dedication

To my friend, Nadine McGill

Gone to soon.

My friend, Nadine, contributed to our first book "What's Self Love Got To Do With It?" in 2018. She loved writing poems and her daughter shared these with me for the world to celebrate Nadine's life. Her words were powerful, and I hope you find the power in them like Nadine and I did.

Pieces of Me All Over the Floor

Scattered and fractured completely ignored
Lost in the shuffle
Scuffled by fear
Wafting and aimless
Is any of me near?
A morsel of memories
A stitch of my soul
A crumb of my confidence
Ambivalence cajoles
"But you are the glue," my self-esteem speaks
"You HAVE to be YOU, there's no time to be weak"
Cluster and muster
Regain and reframe
Synthesize, energize, let go the shame
"I have to be me!" I hear from my heart
No more put asunder

No more pulled apart
To fall apart further I'll not repeat
I'm GRAND who I am
I'm whole I'm complete
By Nadine MCGill

The Goddess Warrior

The goddess warrior emerged, led by her fearless younger self
who never let her forget her power.
She was triumphant at last
having overcome her greatest foe, herself
You see, she had forgotten long ago her true worth,
her infinite value
and had been hoodwinked by her ego into believing
she had been in control all these decades.
But this day, she reigned again.
She regained dominion over her being,
gained sovereignty over her spirit
and released her soul from bondage
back to mastery of herself.
By Nadine McGill

May your wings take you to new places and may you always soar like the angel you are.

Heather

Gratitude

I am grateful for my journey which has crossed paths with the amazing ladies in this book.

I am grateful for my team, my inner circle, and all of you who read this book.

Thank you to Wendie Holbrook, Catherine Saykaly Stevens, Jennifer Traynor, and Lorie Miller Hansen.

May you take one or many lessons and use them to love yourself more.

It is your birthright to have all you dream of.

Heather Andrews, MRT

Compiler, Publisher, 12 X best-selling Amazon Author

www.getyouvisible.com

Table of Contents

Christina Nathalie Smith

Author Christina Nathalie Smith knows both the highs of gaining Olympian status and the lows of discovering she had sustained brain injuries from her extreme sport. She turns adversity into a way to live more consciously, heal, and help others be their best selves. A former World-Class athlete, Christina has reached deep inside herself to tap into the determination that made her successful and helped her conquer the physical, mental, and emotional challenges she experienced in her demanding sports career. Since retiring from bobsleigh, she has translated her competitive spirit and drive into helping other people around the world through her publications, mental coaching, and speaking. Whether you are a young athlete, a coach, an entrepreneur, a business executive, or a parent, Christina's wisdom will spur you on to do better—whether that means finding your purpose in life, overcoming injuries, developing a healthy life beyond transition, or making the world a better place for all. Prepare to be inspired! Gain personal empowerment! Get on the path to greater control of your life!

https://inphone.co/christina

Self Love is committing to self discipline. Making a routine effort towards a daily practice focused on the betterment of one's mind, body and spirit, in order to be optimally conditioned and destined to serve a greater selfless purpose, beyond one's individual needs.

Christina Nathalie Smith

Foreword

The community assembled in this authentic and empowering masterpiece of female authors brings depth, reflection, and inspiration to the spirit. A vast collection of topics from various women from diverse walks of life have vulnerably exposed their lived experiences. These writers know the power of sharing and caring for others, beyond themselves. It is apparent that they understand the profound impact of collaboration and the collective voice. Each unique individual has in some way stepped into the courage to share their exposés within the pages of this candid ensemble.

Purposefully driven and divinely guided by a heart-centered leader, Heather Andrews, and her team have assembled those ready for the task of composition. Bearing heart and soul to eloquently express their story, each a journey like no other. Which one will you resonate with?

Eighteen women of diverse ethnicity, age, and culture from five countries and three continents, have united under a common theme. From tales of strife, loss, illness, victory, depression, self-doubt, divorce and transition, child-rearing, business, and trauma healing, they have been able to manifest a renewed life of inner peace and self-love realized. Each has in their own unique way experienced personal growth and has discovered their untapped potential through confronting their inner demons intrepidly, now inspired to share and become examples to others.

As an Olympian, I understand the power of fear and its ability to disable. One must have faith, face fear, flex and build the "courage muscle" diligently and habitually. Self-love is committing to self-discipline. Making a routine effort towards a daily practice focused on the betterment of one's mind, body, and spirit, in order to be optimally conditioned and destined to serve a greater selfless purpose, beyond one's individual needs. These international women are intrepid warriors who have learned to stand up and face fear, and the inner fight. Once unhappy, hopeless, and discouraged after human struggles, each is now EMPOWERED!

In life, nothing worth having comes easy. These authors have, in their own way, started new chapters in their lives having overcome transformational challenges. These journeys have left them with tools, eye-opening experiences, and life lessons which have elevated their self-worth and esteem. With an awakened inner power, and shining a light bright that was once dim, these now estrogen-revived souls are inspiring, motivating, and generating faith, hope, joy, and celebration from overcoming obstacles once crippling. A distant memory most wanting to be forgotten, however, is now permanently imprinted for the sake of the next generation's learning and building legacy. Individuals called to service, passionate to make an impact, exposing weaknesses, though now making them into strengths; some compelled to go against the norm, rebels or goddesses they could be called. They have followed their heart to bravely share an emotional, spiritual, and physical process on a public canvas. I call them angels within a book of blessings who seek to be the change in the world.

It is an honor to have been asked to share my heartfelt voice! Shine bright fellow Valkyries,

Christina Nathalie Smith, Olympian

Heather Andrews

Heather Andrews: Founder of Get You Visible Publishing, speaker, and 12-time best-selling Amazon author and publisher. She believes in the power of creating your own story and has helped over 200 authors share their unique stories and wisdom with the world, with 45 books published under her company and 26 of them reaching #1 bestsellers.

Heather is the manager and publisher for Womanition for Southern Alberta, whose vision for businesswomen is mentorship growth and visibility. Womanition was the first networking event that she attended after her job restructuring in 2015 and it felt like home. After six years of being a part of this amazing group of women, speaking at events, and being featured in Womanition Magazine, Heather is excited about what this group is creating for the women of Alberta. For her, this journey has been about friendships, business empowerment, creating influence, and impact.

https://linktr.ee/heatherlandrews

Introduction - A New Perspective of Self-Love

By Heather Andrews

It's okay to choose you!

Imagine standing in your kitchen making breakfast like you have done for many years for your family and your partner, then you say something you can't take back, and you meant it so you can't even apologize for saying what you did.

I was married for 25 years till that fateful day, August 11, 2019, when my husband came downstairs that Sunday morning, gave me a kiss on the forehead, and walked away. On that day it felt like the kiss of the end. Nobody died that day except the life we knew as a family.

The words came tumbling out of my mouth, "I don't want to be married anymore." He heard me and turned around to look at me. He said, "I know we have had some rough patches but you don't mean that." My soul was screaming, "Yes, I do!" I was done. I was empty. I was alone. Yes, he loved me but it wasn't enough anymore. It was no one's fault; we had become complacent. I changed and he did not.

I felt so alone when I crawled into bed at night, so if I felt that way, I may as well live that way.

He reacted, but who wouldn't? I had just turned his world upside down.

I knew I had to lead with love. I did not want a fight in court. Our children were older and the house could be his. I did not care. I wanted out. My biggest lesson was that I wanted my adult kids to know that they could break up if they were unhappy in relationships but do it in a healthy way.

I was independent and could regain my footing financially.

If I had known then what I know now, I would have done things a little differently and asked for my half of the house. I earned that. The bottom line is I did not love myself enough to claim what was mine.

The lesson was a rollercoaster to learn.

I had loved myself throughout many segments of my life but on that fateful day that I ended my marriage, I did so because I had to choose myself; no one was going to save me from the emptiness I felt except me. When I shared my experiences with other women, they had felt the same way or their spouses had left. Regardless, it caused emotional pain for all parties that left or were left. It was a journey to identify yourself as a single woman. How did I feel about my life, my choices, how people perceived me, and forgiveness? Do I forgive myself or ask to be forgiven? I had all of these questions but at the core, I realized I loved myself enough to model a different path. Despite my marital status, I was a good woman; a loving one with a huge heart who deserved the best life had to offer. As I connected with more women, I felt compelled to bring these self-love stories to life.

This book has 19 amazing beautiful raw stories of soulful women who learned to love themselves during times of adversity and unhappiness. They loved themselves enough to use their love stories to propel a different road for themselves to create a life they love. When you read these stories, I know that you will find a piece of yourself in each of them. I encourage you to reflect on each story and ask yourself some questions at the end of each chapter.

The lessons I learned during my divorce were:

1. It is okay to be on my own.

2. I can guide my kids to love both of us and encourage a relationship with each of us.

3. Create space for yourself in this world where you can find peace of mind.

4. Find your passion as it lets your mind be at ease.

5. Get comfortable with money. It is wonderful to have it, desire more of it, and be best friends with it. Create an abundant mindset.

6. There are many versions of family, not just the traditional one.

7. I loved myself and was brave enough to ask for something different.

8. I am the creator of my own story.

9. Finding my voice was key.

10. Not blaming someone else for my feelings.

11. Follow your gut every time.

I was blessed to be surrounded by family and friends who held space for me. The journey back has been a trail of honesty as I had to look at myself in the mirror many times and shift my beliefs. Yet, the journey back was actually a journey forward into a life of love, and a better relationship with myself, my ex-husband, and our kids, which is now solid because we lead with love.

My wish for you as you read this book is to find a bit of inspiration, insight, and more love for you so that you know you can ask for what you want and desire, and lead a life on your terms to be the creator of your self-love story.

Love,

Heather Andrews

Best-selling Author, Publisher, Story Coach, and Speaker

www.getyouvisible.com

Amber Louise

Vivacious, passionate, and dedicated to helping others, Amber Louise is an inspiration to many, and a strength to others. As the mother of two teenage boys, she has held many roles, including taxi driver, confidant, chef, and travel agent. In her professional career, Amber works alongside entrepreneurs helping them to realize their goals. She has a diverse portfolio working with numerous clients from large multinational corporations to not-for-profits and solopreneurs. Surrounding herself with experts, Amber has had the opportunity to learn and excel in many areas. In addition to her role as a business coach, she is also a certified nutrition coach and a lover of wine, good food, and the great outdoors. With a great sense of adventure, Amber is not afraid to explore the unknown. She pushes herself, expanding her boundaries and creating opportunities to grow and learn along the way.

Connect with Amber:

https://www.linkedin.com/in/amber-piche/
amberlouise.ca
amber@ambrosiaevents.ca

Chapter 1

Trust Yourself: The Ultimate Form of Self-Love

By Amber Louise

I asked myself if I was making the right decision. I questioned my integrity, my self-worth, and my love for others. I wondered if I was being selfish or self-righteous. I questioned the love I had for my children. I asked myself if the decision I was about to make would be the right decision five months from now, a year from now, and five years from now. The answer was YES; I trusted myself. I know that the decisions I make today are the right decisions for the future I want.

During my life, I have applied this mindset to many tough decisions, some of which include: resigning from a job, starting a business, disciplining my children, booking a trip, and purchasing a vehicle. I have not always been successful in trusting myself, and for many years, I relied on others to make the right decision on my behalf. Although this sometimes worked in my favor, other times it did not. As the years passed and the number of candles on my cake continued to increase, I searched deep within to find the courage to trust myself. When I recount very specific moments in life having independently made the right decisions without any regrets, and compare those to the moments when my voice was overshadowed or manipulated, I sometimes wonder how each outcome may have been different if I had made the decision independently, and without the strong influence or guilt related to the choice that was ultimately made. I recognize that there are moments in life when we must compromise, but the moments when we bury our instincts while knowing it's not the right decision are the ones that make me wonder if the outcome would've been different if I'd had the courage much sooner to trust myself.

The Act of Trust

In the past, I would have defined self-love differently than I do today. I would have described it as taking time out of my busy schedule to treat myself, whether it was getting a massage or a manicure, buying myself flowers, or reading a book with a glass of wine. In the last few years, I would have described it as spending time doing things I love to do; scrapbooking or spending time with friends, going for a hike, or wine tasting at a local winery—of which there is no shortage of where I live—or better yet, hiking with wine! Although many of these things are important for self-care today, I have a different understanding of self-love, and I believe that it is one of the most important things you can do for yourself: Trust.

In the past year, I have experienced things I have never done before. I suppose that is true every year and during every chapter of our lives, but this year was significant to me in many ways. I watched my son go from dependent on Mom, to completely self-sufficient; I went from cooking and cleaning every day for my husband and two teenage boys, to becoming the recipient; I trained for and ran my first marathon; I experienced an unforgettable vacation with three beautiful and inspiring women; I've had some incredible opportunities through work, and am acutely aware that I can get through anything.

To put my current situation into perspective, more recently I was forced to trust myself with what will probably be classified as one of the most important decisions of my life. After 19 years of marriage, I decided to get a divorce. In hearing this news, many of you might be experiencing mixed feelings, including sadness, skepticism, confusion, anger, a sense of pride, or hopefulness. Many of you at this moment can relate because you've gone through a divorce yourself or you were a child when your parents did. Some of you may be intrigued because you find yourself in a similar situation, and some of you may want to learn more as to not find yourself in my position. Nonetheless, please let me explain that this decision did not come lightly. In 19 years, two people experience a lot of life together and grow and evolve together in unpredictable ways.

Leading up to this decision, I did a lot of self-reflection. I asked myself a lot of questions, including, "Why should I?" and "Why shouldn't I?" I researched different reasons why women get divorced and why women choose not to. For me, the choice was very clear, but I wanted to make sure I wasn't making a decision based on guilt, future ideals of what could be, or selfish reasons that I would later regret. This is where self-love comes in.

To trust in yourself is the highest form of self-love. To not self-doubt; to not be regretful, and to truly be at peace with each decision.

The Value of Values

Raising children brings so many joys and challenges, as I'm sure many of you can relate to. I remember one day in the grocery store, one of my boys was not a happy camper. Arms were flailing and words like, "May I please, Mommy" were not being used. At this moment, an older woman passed by and said, "You are a great Mother." I found this statement to be rather profound. I mean, think about it—my child was attracting quite a bit of negative attention and this woman sincerely wanted me to know I was doing a great job. Over the years, I have come to realize that every phase will pass, every challenge will come to an end, and every decision has pros and cons. I learned to trust myself and to remain confident that each decision I make is the best possible choice I can make at that moment. Trusting myself, and that I am doing what is right with the information I have, has proven to be the way I show myself love.

Naturally, there are decisions that I regret or wish I had done differently, but the reality is that I can't go back and change the past. I can; however, influence the future. Each day, as the opportunity for me to make a decision presents itself, I strive to make choices that will positively influence the future.

As a business coach, I have worked with many entrepreneurs, managers, and C-level executives. One of the first questions I ask when we are discussing their goals is, "What are your values?"

Recently, I asked myself this question, not because I've never identified my values before, but because in time, one's values can evolve. As a coach, **my values are to be bold, authentic, and trustworthy.** These three values are true for me as a coach, but also what I encourage in my clients for their businesses. To be bold, we must hold confidence; we must have confidence in ourselves and in what it is we are doing, and we must trust ourselves in that confidence. To be authentic is to know who you are; don't deviate—be true to yourself. And to be trustworthy is to tell it how it is; be kind, compassionate, and show you care, but always tell the truth. In my personal life, I add the **desire to help others** and the value of **happiness.**

I bring up values because it's important to understand the framework from which we should be making decisions. It's important to evaluate each decision against your values and to know that the decisions you make at any given moment are the best ones you can make based on the information you have. Most of the time, you'll be doing this exercise unconsciously, but occasionally, it's important to check in.

For example, I've had many opportunities to work directly for a company versus a contract with two or more companies. **Happiness** is a strong value of mine, and I know having to abide by hourly regiments and asking permission for vacation time is not something that will make me happy, so I've opted for a contract life versus an employee life. I also have an innate **desire to help** others, and when I'm deciding how I spend my time, this value is often a factor.

The desire to help others is prevalent as a strength of mine, too. As per CliftonStrengths, this value of mine is labeled as Individualization. People who are talented in the Individualization theme are intrigued by the unique qualities of each person. According to CliftonStrengths, *"I watch people and talk with them, and when I see opportunities to help them, I do so. I can pinpoint each person's unique interests, strengths, and goals... I am keenly aware of people's unique traits. I believe that I can help individuals deal with problems and take advantage of opportunities. [As well], piece together events and unravel problems."* FN1

Time and time again, when I made decisions that possibly went against the grain, I realized that the decision only "went against the grain" because it didn't line up with someone else's values or desires. The more I trusted in myself to make the right decision for me, the more I noticed that I became increasingly self-confident, more joyful, and happier. As I compounded these decisions over time, my confidence grew, the trust I had in myself grew, and I became more authentic and truer to myself. The more I trusted in myself, the more positive my life became. And thus, I identified that trustworthiness was not only something to stow upon others but also upon myself.

Learning to Trust

I started this conversation around self-love by noting the many experiences I've had this past year, including my son going to college, my living with my parents in my childhood home, and experiencing a vacation of a lifetime. My purpose in sharing some of my most recent experiences is to share that self-love to me today is different than it once was. After some contemplation, I'm not sure I could have defined self-love until recently. Every step along this journey we call life, I've had to make tough decisions, and in doing so, I now realize that I was expressing self-love. Trusting in myself has allowed me to make some tough choices.

For years, I have followed and done what I was told to do. Don't get me wrong, I've always been a strong-willed woman who can stand her ground. However, there was always a level of trust in others that I felt so strongly about that I didn't need to question decisions being made on my behalf. In many situations in my life, this has gone well and produced positive results, but looking back, there are moments when I should have asked myself if I was making the right decision versus relying on someone else to decide for me.

At this point, it might sound like I'm contradicting myself. I am not. Making a decision because you know it is the right choice for yourself and making a decision because you are told it is right are two very different things. I am in a place in my life where I trust myself to make the right decision for the highest and best outcome. I trust myself fully and completely; that is self-love.

Today, if you ask me what self-love is, I'd say: **Self-Love is the ability to trust in myself.** It's the belief I have in myself, knowing I can handle anything thrown at me no matter how many tears I shed or how angry I might get. It's the calm energy and the silent breath I take as I see chaos around me. It's knowing that I can take one more step forward because this is not the end, it is simply part of the journey. No matter what I am going through at the moment, it will pass and a new challenge, fear, or success will be here in no time.

Reframe & Relabel

Deciding to get a divorce is no light decision and will certainly create tremendous life changes. I knew this decision would affect the present and the short-term, and ultimately influence the future for myself, my soon-to-be ex-husband, and our two teenage boys. I was told that this decision would ruin my boys' future and they would not be successful in school, work, or relationships. The fear from others was that in the long run, they would not be successful in life. I was told they had a higher likelihood of getting a divorce, and the best gift I could give them would be to stick it out, repent my sins (of asking for a divorce), and fix my marriage. But what if this was not true? What if the decision to divorce my husband was the right decision, and if I didn't do this, my boys would grow up to see what an unhealthy relationship looked like?

You see, the reality is that I'll never know, nor will they. My boys will only know their new reality—that they are the children of divorced parents. But what happens if we reframe this comment?

What about instead of labeling them as victims, we label them as the strong, driven, resilient, and caring individuals that they are? What if we say they are the children of two loving parents; the children of a truly happy mom who smiles and laughs with them, and understands what it is to be joyful? What if they are witnesses to successful parents in their respective careers because space allowed for this to happen? What if they feel love and joy in a different way because they have two loving homes that they can spend time in and learn from? And thus, I circle back to my current reality; that I am making the right decision at the moment with the information that I have on hand. I can foreshadow the future all I want, but the only thing I can actually do is attempt to influence the future and hope that I do it positively.

Committed to Becoming a Better Version of Myself

Over the last 20 years of my career, I have watched myself grow as a professional woman, a mother, a daughter, a sister, and a coach. While in university, I started my first business, a hospitality staffing company. I hired 12 people, trained them to serve in a banquet environment, and was then hired by a 4-star hotel and one of the top wineries in Canada. When I graduated from university, I closed that company and started a career in marketing.

A few years later, I started a tea company, which was one of my husband's ideas. People still ask me today, "Why tea?" I had an answer for them, but in reality, the answer was because my husband said so. This was one of those things I was told to do rather than decided to do. Don't misinterpret me, I agreed to start the company, but it was more so out of the fact that I was told it was the right decision versus deciding it was the right decision. I didn't ask many questions because I simply trusted him. I had a full-time job at the time, so during lunch hours, evenings, and weekends, I spent hundreds of hours doing market research and developing the brand. Six months later, and exactly two weeks after my first son was born, we launched the tea company at a local craft fair. For the next 15 years, I ran the tea company off the side of my desk. We made very few profits, but I learned a f**k-ton. In these same 15 years, I advised many friends and other working professionals about how they should run their businesses, market their products and generate sales, fail fast, and pivot. I was a stay-at-home mom, a working professional, and a self-proclaimed guru of business. Friends and family would ask me business questions, and so would friends of friends, parents of kids from the boys' school and sports teams, as well as peers in the business community. Most of the time I did it because I cared and wanted to help, and some of the time I did it for pay. But at the end of the day, I had the desire to learn and to help.

Another one of my strengths is that I love to learn. I am constantly asking questions, researching something, and trying to better understand. As per CliftonStrengths, *"I think systematically to identify patterns in processes, data, facts, relationships… I see distinct linkages between this factor and that consequence, this decision and that result, or this action and that reaction. People trust me to make informed and reasonable choices. They are likely to ask what I think before they finalize a plan or state their position."* FN2

Over the years, I found myself taking on more of a leadership role and advising more so than doing. Today, I work with over fifty companies by helping them to expand and grow their businesses. I am constantly learning about business, but also about myself.

I aspire to be the best version of myself every day and am committed to sharing my experiences with others. Similarly, to the analogy of a kitten looking in the mirror and seeing the reflection of a lion, my goal is to be "the lion" and the inspiration that reflects back to others. I work hard and play hard; I enjoy going to the gym the same as I enjoy a glass of wine with friends. I enjoy going for a hike carrying an extra 25lb weight vest the same as I enjoy listening to a client share their most recent work or life challenge. I enjoy foods that some would consider unhealthy and spend too much time staring at a screen, but I love myself, love where I'm at, and I truly trust myself. I would consider my life to be very well-balanced, which at the end of the day is what I think we are all striving for.

Many years ago, I remember a story of a woman who did a boudoir photoshoot for her husband. When the photos had been taken, she asked the photographer to smooth out the wrinkles, erase the stretch marks, and thin out a few areas. When she shared the edited photos with her husband, he was disappointed, saying that those are the things that make her who she is. The wrinkles show wisdom, the stretch marks show that she is a mother, and the love rolls show that life happens. This story has always reminded me to be comfortable in my own skin and to appreciate all the imperfections because they tell the story of who I have become. Although I strive to be a better version of myself each day, I don't discount who I am today and the journey I took to get here.

The wonderment of the physical body amazes me. With my body, I have climbed mountains, nourished myself and others, shared a loving embrace, made love, made babies, and artistically created amazing things. I have also encouraged others to live a healthier lifestyle by being a good example to them. I exercise regularly and often push myself. I eat a healthy diet but never fret about the cookie or chips I consume. I am careful with my words. When I listen to others, I listen with the intent to "hear" rather than to just respond. I try to give them the benefit of the doubt and do my best to prevent them from feeling defensive. I have also laughed until I've peed and cried myself to sleep. I pride myself on being a good example of balance between work and play, as well as self-love and self-discipline. Every day, I am reminded that I am a role model to my boys, my brothers, their girlfriends/wives, my parents, my extended family, my friends, their children, my clients, my peers, my neighbors, and myself. Trusting myself is the greatest reward I can receive and the greatest gift I can give.

Self-love can sometimes be perceived as a tricky topic. Some people hear the term self-love and they think you are being selfish. Some think that if you have self-love, you care for others less or that you don't care for others at all. When we make a conscious decision to have self-love, we are in reality, then able to share the best version of ourselves with others.

I believe as women, we each have so much inner and outer beauty. Sometimes we may have a hard time seeing the beauty in ourselves or others, but I tell you it is there. As daughters, sisters, friends, mothers, leaders, and role models, we must each embrace our truth, which is in part that we are incredible humans, but more so, that we can make decisions and trust ourselves in doing so. This belief comes from within each of us.

Learn to love yourself. Be confident in the skin you are in; be confident with the knowledge you have. Strive to be a better person, a better friend, a better mother, daughter, sister, a better wife or partner, and a better lover. Having the confidence to trust yourself is potentially the most important gift you can give yourself.

FN1 – GALLUP | CliftonStrengths | An Introduction to the Individualization CliftonStrengths Theme | ***https://www.gallup.com/cliftonstrengths/en/252272/individualization-theme.aspx***

FN2 – GALLUP | CliftonStrengths | An Introduction to the Learner CliftonStrengths Theme | ***https://www.gallup.com/cliftonstrengths/en/252293/learner-theme.aspx***

BONUS: How to Identify your Values

List out 3-5 people that you highly respect or have high regard for.

____

____

____

____

____

List out 3-5 people whom you consider to be your best friends.

____

____

____

____

____

List out 3-5 people whom you do not respect and/or do not like.

____

____

____

____

____

For the first group, people you highly respect, list out all the reasons why you respect them.

___

___

___

___

___

For the second group, people whom you consider to be your best friends, list out all the reasons why.

___

___

___

___

___

Do you see a pattern? Are there any phrases or words you have listed that you resonate with? What are some terms that describe you or that you would like to describe yourself?

For the third group, people you do not respect, list out the reasons why.

___

___

___

___

___

The list of reasons you've identified from the third group most likely includes the opposite terms from your first and second lists. Are there any surprises here?

From these three lists, write out the words or phrases that most resonate with you. You should have about 10-15.

____

____

____

____

____

Can you combine any of these terms? (For example fun, joy, and happiness are similar. Is there one that resonates stronger with you?)

List out 3-5 of your top Values

____

____

____

____

____

Congratulations! You have identified your top personal values.

Lessons Learned

1. Self-love is not selfish. Trusting yourself is the greatest gift you can give yourself. Trustworthiness is not only something to stow upon others but also upon yourself. ***To trust yourself is the highest form of self-love.*** To not self-doubt, and to not be regretful, but to truly be at peace with each decision. When we make a conscious decision to have self-love, we are then able to share the best version of ourselves with others.
2. It's important to ensure you are making the right decision for yourself and not just listening to what others deem to be the right decision for you.
3. In life, we are on a journey. Every phase will pass, every challenge will come to an end, and every decision has pros and cons. It's important to understand that life is not stagnant but constantly flowing. You will never have all of the information, but you will have enough to make the best possible decision at the moment.

Mindset Tips

1. Your values are what drive every decision you make, whether consciously or unconsciously. Identify your values and check in with them once in a while.
2. There is a difference between making a decision because you are ***told*** it is the right one and making a decision because you ***know*** it is the right one. Make sure you make decisions that you know are right for you.
3. You can't change the past, but you can reflect upon it, learn from it, and make a conscious effort to influence the future. This simple action will allow you to work towards making decisions that will positively influence the future.

Aha Moments and Self-Reflections

Note your Thoughts

Andrea Petrut

Andrea Petrut is a fierce advocate for healing, self-empowerment, and love. These threads are always woven into her personal life as well as in speaking, writing, coaching, mentoring, and teaching. Her own journey of self-discovery, self-love, and empowerment is behind her work in the world. Wherever she lived, in Romania and Canada, she has been her own pillar in life, lifting herself and others on her path. When people take agency and open their hearts to remembering and embracing their uniqueness, she lightens up because she believes that we are all born one and we are all connected—something she experienced and remembered from childhood—and every little change we make will benefit others too. Andrea is on a mission to guide compassionate changemakers to lead with their spirituality, serving for the highest good of all.

Connect with Andrea:

https://andreapetrut.ca/

Chapter 2

Remembering the Sacred

By Andrea Petrut

It was the spring of 2015. I was 34 years old and looking through the balcony windows at poplars, oaks and acacias. My boys, ages seven and three, were living with me in a cozy rented apartment on the third floor of an old building in my hometown, Galați, in Romania, minutes away from the Danube River cliff, playgrounds, willows, the port and promenades. That sunny day was bathing me in a warm light—a healing moment, one of many, after many years of traumas, hurtful experiences, and unhealthy relationships. As I watched the breeze moving the branches and the sun cheering me on, I accepted the truth: I was a married woman raising two boys alone, supported financially by my ancestors, my father, and the little I could make on my own. I put myself in that situation and now wonder: *Why have I never pondered on my own beliefs and views on relationships and family life? Why have I never questioned my own perceptions, or never gained clarity and asked myself what really mattered to me?* I didn't have a clear idea of what kind of family fulfilled me. I used to decide impulsively without looking back and learning my lessons, without having my values, principles and boundaries clear, and without looking ahead and thinking of legacy and how I would want to lead my way. I just said yes to whatever felt more comfortable, safe, or doable for me. All the decisions I made like that had a steep price that almost cost me my life a few times. I was an over-giver who thought sacrificing her own well-being was worth it. Frankly, I didn't even count myself in. I put others first and me last so much that I became overwhelmed by the responsibilities and stress I had put on myself and reached the end of the line more than once. The subconscious beliefs that led me to experience all that began many years ago.

I was born in Romania at the beginning of the last decade of the Communist regime. The events in 1989 (the coup d'état) with over a thousand innocents dead (the youngest being a one-month-old baby), four times more wounded and no terrorist in sight, traumatized us all, millions of different generations who were alive that day. Our town was not a hot spot of the "revolution," and we were not directly affected, so my family could make the transition to a different life—the so-called democracy—which was easier than for other people. Or so it seemed. Who knows what's underneath the smiling faces, celebrations, and holidays in the mountains? Who can tell what is deep within someone's body and soul every day unless they share or we have the ability to ask and listen? Clearly my father and I didn't know because we missed what probably started in 1991. *She wouldn't tell until it became obvious.* In 1992, my mother got so sick that she couldn't hide it anymore and had to go to the hospital. The doctors discovered she had stage 3 stomach cancer—simple words without meaning for me. During my first visit at the hospital, I had an insight that she would die and that was the day that changed my life forever. I was 11 years old.

Slowly and surely, though also pretty fast if you asked me, the cancer built trenches in her body, spreading its poison cell by cell, unnoticeable on the outside while gripping on the inside, taking over her strength, her energetic presence, and her spark. At first, she was still able to move around. Gradually, she was stuck inside walls, and then glued to a bed. If hell had sounds, surely, they would have been my mother's screams for death to come sooner when not even morphine would enter her body to soothe her pain. "The silent killer" wasn't so silent after all. Death came at a shocking moment for us, her loved ones. Hopefully, peace came over her, as she died in her sleep. She became an ancestor.

A seed was planted as I watched life leave my mother day by day: *If you want to leave a legacy, make sure you are present in your life to give moments where others can enjoy, receive, or share something with you so the world can pass on what you are here to impart.* My mom left me with her smile and attitude, loving hugs, walks, hiking, photos, cards, and memories of times with her—enough to show me love and too little to solve the mystery of who she was and her deepest desires. Why have we forgotten elderhood? Why aren't we appreciating stories in our families? Why don't we give and we don't ask? What will be left of us if those stories are not told and no one knows who we were, where we came from, what we have done, or what has been done to us? I was blessed that my father loved sharing stories and I loved to listen. I didn't have the same opportunities with my mother, though.

Between her diagnosis and her death, I came to be a mature mind in a preteen body. Maybe this was what the Romanian folk stories meant when a character "grew one year like others in seven." Mentally and emotionally, I was on my own. My family was drowning in grief and pain while I was bringing my mom's legacy (the Sunshine) with me, learning how to grow my own light. My review of the last year of her life made me believe that **prevention is better than treating**, and I put that in the back of my mind. This led to my hunger for learning about myself as a human wanting to live a long life in good health. It proved to be a lengthy journey of self-discovery, self-acceptance, acceptance of the reality I lived in, self-compassion, and self-love.

My loved ones continued their lives heartbroken and dealing with loss in their specific way. I pulled through it by hiding my pain under anger and grief, numbing myself under a shield of unbeatable willpower, and walls of determination to stay alive until my own descendants would be old enough to be on their own. *I believed my mother could have prevented her illness and prolonged her life. I believed she had a choice.* Whether she could have or not, I'll never know. **My deeper belief became that there are things we can control in our life.** Thus began my quest to find what those things are.

I turned into a traumatized girl, armored and ready to face life as it was. Very deep within, under the shields, I knew from lived experience who was my supporter, my loving source, my protection and guide: Spirit, the Higher Power, God. Those days of hidden grief continued with loving showers of reality, awakening moments from life through friends and colleagues, love and support, all bringing change for the better. While I became stubborn in ways that didn't serve me, I also kept one helpful thing—the will and determination of a warrior following the Light, the Higher Power as the guiding North Star and wanting to reach the Star itself, the Source, without holding on to what I could lose anytime—my family, friends, body, and material things. The ability to detach myself so much had its drawbacks; I didn't always appreciate nor cared for what I had. Decades had to pass to learn to hold different perspectives at once while living in harmony.

Hence spirituality became from my early years a wellspring of strength, abundance, filling my experiences with beauty, wonder, fun, play, learning, wisdom, both in daytime and nighttime, and miracles. Whenever I put myself in danger or risky situations, something came up and miracles happened, or by some divine intervention, I had moments of clarity and listened to my gut or intuition. I could go through very harsh situations because I had something to hold on to; something to bring me back to myself, to sanity, and to reality. When I forgot about my roots or my own resources, life had its ways of waking me up from my own paralysis and reminding me of my why and purpose.

My pursuit for the meaning of life and the things we can change became the bridge between my spiritual life and my interest in health and wellness. The practices that attracted me most involved breathing, internal organs, musculoskeletal system, singing, prayer, and being mindful of nutrition, thoughts, and emotions. Whether it was Yoga, Tai Chi, Chi Kung, Shaolin Kung Fu, stretching, singing in the church or at home, dancing, relaxation techniques or fitness, playing piano or guitar, or drawing; everything was a mix of two or more aspects of myself. Self-development and self-actualization one way or another made me involve all parts of who I am so I couldn't ignore the body. But my view on the body was first that of an outsider looking at a separate entity, inside-out while also outside-in. I felt and knew I was living in my body and at the same time, I was perceiving my body as a somewhat connected yet extraneous part of me.

It was observation, a skill I used as much as I could from an early age, that helped me train myself to notice physical changes. My body was teaching me through pain, odor, sensations, and emotions. I increased my awareness to know when I had toxins or was sick even before I had clear symptoms. I used self-education and noticing to discover what was normal, what was unusual, and what could be a concern for me. All my learning and education were centered around relationships: my relationship with my body, my emotions, and my mind, as well as my relationship with other people, with movement, with nature, and with the divine. Thus, in high school, I was already involved in self-directed studies on emotions and emotional intelligence, enlightenment, human history and evolution, sacred geometry, creativity, inventions, how the Universe is governed, the divine, higher intelligence, and much more. I exchanged thoughts and ideas with whomever was willing to have conversations with me to learn, study, listen and explore, share and challenge themselves and my thinking.

I played with the ideas of control and self-control and tested them on me and in the relationships where I was challenged most. This game with myself had been my fun time from childhood. I learned how to sneak out from my bedroom after waking up to eavesdrop while my parents chatted over coffee. It also was a great tool for protection in emotionally and mentally difficult situations. My detachment (or emotional un-attachment) became my best friend when guys tried to lure me into intimate relationships that I didn't want.

Despite all the awareness, strong will and self-control, I didn't really care about my body. I didn't love myself. My curiosity and hunger for knowledge and understanding were not enough to go deeper and wider, to get to the core of my issues and who I was, or to love and accept myself. Even the anatomy and biology classes in school were not enough to teach me how to treat myself or how to build a healthy relationship with my body and with those I chose to love and bring into my life. "Wellness" wasn't even a word in the family, among friends, colleagues, or society in general. Health was something to deal with when things went wrong. Prevention was not mainstream. Therapy, trauma release and transformation tools, and coaching were not something normal, desirable and available as we would have later. My body was a mystery to discover and a world to protect. **I was still separated while looking for wholeness.**

I had a combination of ignorance, curiosity and shame towards my physicality. More masculine than feminine, leading my life my way while respecting my family's values as much as I could, I kept my spiritual, unusual or weird experiences to myself as I was afraid not to have pushback or lose very close friends. What I cared about most was that I knew what I lived, and nobody was able to take that from me; it was my truth.

I was ashamed to ask questions about my female body and start conversations. I didn't even know what I was looking for. Magazines and books around my teenage years and beginning of adulthood were helpful, but even they made me question the perspectives presented, and what they were educating the youth (and me, that is). I wanted to explore "me" as a whole, not as a general body or an idea of someone my age and gender.

In my own family, this vessel that carries us each day wasn't something to pay much attention to, though clearly was very important. My life, on the other hand, kept showing me there is more to this unity, communion of cells, and organisms that live in symbiosis than meets the eye, otherwise we wouldn't have needed a body to live in the first place! Studying history through the eyes of witnesses from Holocaust, like Viktor Frankl, or life through those who had near-death experiences (I would later have my own experience with that and it wasn't much like what I read about, by the way), nurtured the truth I felt in my DNA that we are more than body and mind. And I believed wholeheartedly that nobody can take away what we hold in our consciousness, and in our spirit. Therefore, I built a stronger mindset of someone who can put up with a lot because there is something invincible, inalienable, and untouchable in me. I started searching for what that was and how I could live from that space more.

Always from within, during my adventures and experiences, glimpses of the future appeared, like déjà-vus I needed to catch up with. One time, an insight was an image and idea of me being the mother of a girl—that's when I promised myself that I would live until my girl reached adulthood and independence. In a subsequent vision, I was a mother of boys.

Interestingly, motherhood came when I was in a stage of forgetfulness, when I forgot where I was going and why. *I forgot my strengths and divine gifts, my ancestors and my path.* I was repeating the same pattern with toxic relationships: I was either over-giving, sometimes with a motherly attitude that took away people's responsibility for their own actions and life, or accepting to be treated less than I deserved. Actually, I was the one who didn't take responsibility fully for her own life!

Life challenged me to be uncomfortable, see my flaws, and accept what I needed to learn. I had a big ego that covered all that I didn't want to see, hear, sense, or know. While going through unhealthy relationships, I also discovered what's fundamental for me. My children became the eyes of the Universe, teaching me how to thrive. My boys, through their unconditional love, personalities and interactions, unwillingly tested my beliefs, choices, thoughts, and together we learned what matters. I pushed my limits and went beyond anything I could have ever imagined. I became a pioneer in my family; a rule breaker, a challenger, and a trailblazer in parenting and leadership from within.

Motherhood propelled me to discover a whole new world related to health and humanity, not just humans in general. I learned to appreciate each other's role in the community and ask for help. I learned my experience is not alone or separated but part of "one." I shared so others who have lived through similar experiences could know better, do better, and get better results.

When it was hard, I remembered my upbringing. My mother modelled womanhood, leadership and dignity. I recalled what a woman like her was capable of in her life and community. My father was the one who modelled integrity, independence, co-leadership, and true friendship. Of course, absorbing values and implementing them takes time, but the seeds were inside. One day, I would embody all.

There was still more for me to learn before I could lead my life to my best and highest interest. At first, I entrusted others with my well-being. Gradually, encounters with different people over time, including doctors, taught me that trust is not something to take or give lightly. It finally occurred to me that I couldn't trust all the people I loved because it takes will (thus choice), responsibility, deep practice and dedication to become honest with oneself and others, and to have integrity and show up in service for the highest good. That's when I felt those around me were not as connected as I was with my heart, my path and my calling. Even if I didn't know much about me and life, at least I cared. I cared about myself. I didn't see myself as mere systems, mechanical, and predetermined components in a complex environment. We, as humans, tend to erase what is most beautiful of us and invite all that bears no fruit, no aliveness, no soul, no heart, no connection within us, with ourselves, with each other, with nature, or with the world itself. I was determined to find what's beyond the paradigms that felt false and bring it out so others could see it, acknowledge it and connect with it.

That day in 2015, I took agency. I got out of hiding by looking at the truth and trusting I would be fine. I reconnected with God, the divine source, my lifelong friend and guide, and asked for help and clarity, and started taking action steps to reveal the answers. I turned my life around by ending old stories, searching for deep transformation and awareness, looking into changing my environment (thus my beliefs), and building a future where I became the leader I was born to be.

Seven years later, I'm in my bedroom looking out the window, bathed in unconditional love from the Universe, nourished by the nature around me, held by all the many soulful relationships that I have built in Canada and all over the world. My heart is filled with joy, and my soul is shining. My life is a series of synchronicities and flow. The vision I was given for my second husband (Gabriel, my match, "the one") and I is fulfilling. I am grateful for being alive, for who I am now, all I've done and become, all that I have and I don't have, for the journey of my life, for my ancestors and the wisdom I keep receiving. The pine trees and buildings in front of me stand tall while they allow me to see a clear sky, the sun shining above them, and downtown Toronto in the distance. I am at peace in a rented townhouse, a space suitable for a family like mine, in a hospitable and safe neighborhood. December 2022 will be five years that I've lived in Canada, happily married with three bundles of joy (my biological children, including a girl). This feels like a déjà-vu.

Exercise

Take deep breaths until you feel calm and settled within. See your life as a series of stories, flowing like springs into a big river. Which feels more vibrant, more alive to you? Which has more light, shine or sparkle in your mind, heart, and body? Jot down the most important and memorable elements or keywords from those images, colors, energies, or however you see, sense, feel, or are aware of these stories. Pick one story you feel more attracted to. Where did you love yourself more and how? Have you ever felt loved, cared for, seen, heard, valued, or appreciated? What was that like? Where in your body did you feel that? Were you able to hold it? Did you lose it? How? Can you bring it back? How would you live that now? How can you take your own experience and make it the foundation for a new life, a fulfilling one, where you matter and you start feeling whole?

Lessons from my life:

1. Life is a bucket full of strength to hold us until our time is done. Accept the journey from A to B and live wholeheartedly, present in every moment, loving and receiving love, and life replenishes, and is fulfilling.

2. Self-love means coming to self and returning to the sacred. Our body was given to us, a conduit for our expression, living in fulfilment, joy, love, and stepping into the vision we bring into the world. As a leader in all aspects of my life, personal and business, as a visionary and compassionate changemaker, I have learned that loving myself means I choose:

- my own body's wellness
- to live in a way that serves me the most on my path
- the relationships that help me on my journey
- to take and keep the strongholds in my ancestry and see what needs healing and transformation from the rest in order to embrace them all and change our stories

3. True change comes from within, going deep into the beliefs, patterns, stories, and wisdom, including the legacy of our ancestors and shifting from there.

Aha Moments and Self-Reflections

Note your Thoughts

Brittnie Hamilton

Brittnie Hamilton is a woman on a mission to help others become unshakeable in their confidence, and master overcoming fear of judgment and limiting beliefs. She stepped into the coaching world to help others shift their mindset while unequivocally overcoming any judgment or unworthiness after all her healing and growth in self-love. Her passion has always been to help people feel their best, which she mastered in her seventeen years as a hairstylist. Listening to others' stories, hearing their hearts, and lifting them up is the passion she embodies and loves dearly because helping on a bigger, deeper level becomes more and more clear.

Brittnie is a momma to three children who are at the center and purpose of all she does. She is married to her best friend, who has walked alongside her through her remarkable self-love journey, and they live happily in Colorado. Journaling, walking, hiking, camping, paddle boarding, and working out are Brittnie's favorite spare time activities.

Connection with Brittnie:

hello@brittniehamilton.com
https://www.instagram.com/brittnie_hamilton/
www.facebook.com/thebrittniehamilton

Chapter 3

Orange Wasn't My Color

By Brittnie Hamilton

I stood there as a 22-year-old shell of myself, and learned that I was facing 12-24 years behind bars as the judge spoke to me. I thought about running, or maybe just dealing with it, or fighting like hell to change the outcome. I realized then that I had a choice and I'd better decide quickly.

Thinking back to that night, I had never been in trouble before, never been arrested, and for sure never been to jail. When the officer read me my rights and placed me under arrest for vehicular homicide, I thought my life was over.

It was a Friday night, and I had been doing an apprenticeship for my career at the time, finally reaching the end of a long day. I had a couple drinks like most 22-year-olds do on the weekends. I had to run an errand; I was returning a movie that I kept getting charged late fees for. I couldn't afford all the daily fees and finally had the time to take it back. I know now that the price I was going to pay for returning it was going to be much higher than what that movie rental ever was. I was almost back home, where I lived with roommates and my boyfriend, when everything changed in a flash of a moment. I saw the car next to me slam on their brakes, as if in slow motion, and as they slowed, he appeared. There was a man in the street, in the middle of the road and not at a crosswalk, with no light on him and it was pitch black. I slammed on my brakes but it was too late. He kept walking and my car didn't stop. The next thing I knew to do was to get help for him. It was in that moment life stood still—life was about to change.

In the days that followed, things were a whirlwind. I moved back home with my mom, spoke with attorneys (which I never thought I'd need to do in my life), and was hitting a major depression for all that had happened. As I sat on the bed in my room, my mom came in to speak with me. You see, my mom was the most loving, supportive, and encouraging woman; she was my rock and only showed me love and protection growing up. But she was a woman of few, yet strong and impactful, words, so when she started to talk, I realized I better listen up. "Brittnie, you have two choices right now: You can stay in here, let this completely destroy you, and throw your life away, or you can turn this into a redemption for who you truly are, who you want to become, and come out better and stronger." We both knew at this point that prison was a heavy weight of what my life was going to look like. Someone died and I was the one driving the car. We had found out shortly after through friends and law enforcement that the man in the street had been talking of suicide that day and had just left a nearby bar with his friend. They both had stopped on the side of the road, waiting for cars to pass when the man I had hit decided to walk out into oncoming traffic; he was playing Russian roulette with vehicles, and that's when our paths crossed in tragedy.

A year later, we were in court and that's when my family and boyfriend stood behind me as I waited to find out my sentence. I had never been more nervous, more terrified, or more remorseful in my life. My hands were sweaty, and I remember being so weak in the knees, like I was almost having an out of body experience as I waited to hear my sentence. Six years in maximum security prison was the final decision. I had a brief moment to hug my family goodbye and then embark on a journey I had only seen played out in movies. This was when I took my mom's words and knew no matter where I was going to end up, I'd become the best version of myself possible.

I told my boyfriend at the time, who is now my husband, that we should just be friends. I was in love with him, and loved his support and friendship, but to wait that amount of time for your girlfriend at such a young age just didn't seem right or fair to him. We had traced our hands on paper and sent them in the mail once I was gone so we could hold hands and pray together every night. We were hopeful and prayed for an appeal to change my sentence, but the time for that was unknown. It could be weeks, months, or years; we didn't know the timeline. Finally, my court appeal date ended up coming quicker than we thought. Six months later, to be exact. I asked him why he stayed with me, and why he was going to stand before the judge on my behalf to plead for my sentence to be changed or reduced. This was his response:

> Regarding our relationship, I considered for a long time what would come of it. It's one that I sought for years, and the one I'd been yearning for a lifetime to behold. Why stick around in a show of support? Why orate to the open court on her behalf? Why not run away and forget that this piece of my life even happened? Faith. That's it. Despite the naysayers, the haters, the future hardships this would inevitably bring, my faith was redeemed and we have been restored time and again. I'm so thankful for the family we've made and the life we've built, but without faith in God, none of this would have been possible. His faithfulness rebuilt our relationship, and taught us both the importance of planning and purpose in our relationship both then and now.

To this day, I can never thank him enough for the support, love and grace he showed me through that time. He truly believed in me when I wasn't too sure of myself, and didn't feel worthy of love. I never thought we'd be where we are.

In early June in my cell, six months into my sentence, a guard knocked at my door and the words he said took me what felt like an hour to process: "Pack your bags. You leave tomorrow." What? I had no idea what he was talking about because I'd been sentenced to six years. I had only served six months of my sentence, and figured he had gotten something wrong. Little did I know the appeal decision came back and I was going to a six-year outpatient facility. I was going home and this was my second chance.

While I was away for six months, I really started to learn a different and deeper level of myself. I thought about who I truly wanted to become and who I wanted to help after this. I learned there could be a duality for being strong in the moment of my sentence, and also praying and working towards things outside that moment for a better life. I learned that there is truly no limit to what prayer and believing in yourself is capable of. I learned that one moment and a bad decision doesn't define you or need to hold you back from the life you were meant to lead. I learned that the power of your being is in your hands, and things you want in life are all possible if you're willing to go for it. I learned one of the biggest things was the ability to forgive and love myself, and to know my worth. An almost bigger lesson was to allow others to love me fully and unconditionally, and to know I was worthy of all things outside of this piece of my story. I knew in my deepest being that I had a purpose, and planned to help others see that by virtue of their humanity, they were worthy of growth, self-love and able to relinquish fear of judgement.

As I look back to the girl that I was, I can see all that I had to overcome in order to grow and have the ability to finally believe in myself. I would repeat a verse daily that I still hold close when I need that extra strength or courage: *"I can do all things through Christ who strengthens me," Philippians 4:13*. This was the scripture that really brought me hope, and it gave me the courage to continue in life after what had happened. It brought me to a pivotal point where I knew I'd never be alone, even in the moments when I felt unworthy or fearful of judgement from others.

You may ask how did I get from there to here? How did I learn to come out of one of my darkest moments? How was I going to grow into someone I would be proud of and evolve into the best version of myself?

I truly believe that it's in the darkest moments where more strength, grit, and beauty really can come to life. It is where your personal power and resilience come into play and help you to land on your feet. When I came home after my sentence and had six more years of outpatient monitoring and rehabilitation, I knew I could take the darkness and bring it to light. I knew I had to work through and process the hurt, trauma, anger (at myself), and self-doubt, and look at the bigger plan. I had a choice to rebuild my life and find love for myself again.

How would you go from a six-year prison sentence to being given a second chance? Would you beat yourself up for what happened? Would you forgive yourself for your part in it? Would you believe that you were never worthy of a happy, good life ever again? Would you be ashamed every time you saw people who knew your story? Would you ever get out of the shame, guilt and pain for all you caused? These are just the surface of emotions I felt. I was in a fight or flight state for a long time, just staying on course with the courts and legally doing everything right. But it was the emotional and mental changes during that time that really placed me on a path that I will forever be grateful for.

There were steps and tools I had to learn to be able to heal and continue on. These are things I still use to strengthen my belief in myself; to know self-love and to know I'm worthy of my life now.

The pain and trauma I caused in one night was like a spider web. I could spot the main parts where I hurt people; I knew the impact on my family and his family, but the small slivers of the web barely seen were deep and spread to people I had never even met. The courage to bounce back from that and find my worth was a journey, and one I had to climb deeply out of.

I started realizing I needed a roadmap to loving myself and my life again. I needed to re-energize who I was and who I wanted to be. I had to start guarding my mind from bullies (the biggest one being myself) and learning it was a powerful tool. Your mind is your biggest asset; it can be your best friend and cheerleader, or it can be the tool to destroy you. We all have a tape that plays in our mind in certain situations. Mine was on autopilot of bad self-talk, unworthiness, and overthinking to an extreme. I was in a place where I had to reinvent the song that I was playing. I started small by becoming aware and honest in the quiet moments of how I talked to myself. I started analyzing and becoming curious of what I was depositing into my beliefs. Once I realized my go-to verbiage of negative self-talk, it was time to change it. I'll never forget the day I fully understood how to tap into this. I was walking to a counselor session on a sunny day, and I remember exactly what I was wearing. I had on jeans, a brown frilly tank top, and my gold flip flops. I could hear the birds as my mind was opening up to the idea of how I was speaking to myself. It was on this day that I recall so clearly what was happening. I was finally connecting to myself on a deeper level, and understanding the power of my mind.

When negative self-talk would pop up, especially when I was alone, I learned to not let the full tape I was feeding myself continue to play. I stopped it dead in its tracks and changed the tune of the song. For example, in my mind I'd say to myself,

"You will never be loved deeply again and you don't deserve a happy life after all that's happened." I got to a point where I'd hear myself and stop after "you will," then change the narrative to "You will forever be a child of God and He loves you exponentially." Stopping these thoughts in their tracks helped me to eventually stop going there. I was able to recreate the paths in my brain to help me heal. I was able to use my strongest tool and reshape the direction that my life could lead.

Tell me that's not great news! You can retrain your brain! You can create positive thinking habits rather than feeling like you're stuck with any thoughts that are not serving you. To me, this was different from affirmations because saying affirmations are an intentional way of looking at the positive. However, this was changing the negative dialogue at that moment and changing the path of where our minds can go. I was giving myself love and grace.

So, what's the soundtrack you're playing in your mind? Is it positive, and is it serving you? Is it lifting you up? If not, there's a tool to redirect it, though you need to become aware and in tune with your self-talk, and become honest with what you want in life. You are so capable of changing the beliefs, thoughts, and direction of your life and the path it's on; it all starts with the thoughts in your mind and aligning them with your heart.

I also learned that a process for me to have self-love again was to have overall wellness within myself. I believe that a love for healing had to happen emotionally, physically, and spiritually. I found hiking and walks satisfied and enhanced this tremendously. There was a way to fill these three cups all within one activity. You see, being outside and connecting with nature gave me such a boost of happiness, and this freeing, disconnection from the noise of life. There is something about the sun shining down, birds chirping, and having nature under your footsteps; something about being outside, getting exercise, and clearing the mind. The power of connection to your body, and breathing as you are engaging in a physical activity is so powerful. I realized though, quite quickly, what I loved the most was going on walks or hikes with no distractions. I liked going alone, but I also would walk in silence, no headphones, no music, podcasts, or anything that would pull me away from rebalancing. The remarkable thing was that in the quiet while walking outdoors, I really connected with my higher power. It's so crazy to me that with all the noise around us all the time, and all that we take in and consume, it's the small moments that have the biggest impact and greatest lesson. God held me so tightly as I grew through and processed so much. He gave me the strength to stay quiet so that I could hear or see the message I was meant to get. He gave me the courage to love myself when there were trials of unworthiness. For me, this wellness triangle, as I call it, is the physical, spiritual, and emotional collaboration with being outdoors that has helped me love life and myself again.

I have to tell you that after the negative self-talk and the emotional healing with a flare of exercise, I had to confront my biggest obstacle. I had to face the piece that I battled with; the piece that was the hardest to accept. I had to learn how to let someone love me to the fullest. I needed to work on feeling worthy of living again, and let go of the pain of judgment I feared. I had to realize that my past didn't define me and that I was deserving of a life full of all the blessings. This was my big hill to conquer, and the monster that kept me pushing people away. I was playing small, even though I had done all the mind work to grow. It was letting someone else say whether I was worthy of love, appreciation, and to have full support and encouragement. I don't know why my beliefs used to put such a block on the allowance of being loved. I would self-sabotage, push people away, purposely disconnect, and put walls up.

I'm so thankful to my husband and my mom for giving me the space to figure this piece out. When you have moments of self-doubt, unworthiness, and those dark valleys where you don't know if you'll climb out, that's when you need to lean in even stronger to God and the ones around you. Looking back, I realize that this journey was not about family and friends loving me more, or them working harder to show me that I'm worthy. [1] It came from me loving them enough to finally heal and love myself. I had to dig deep to heal wounds of feeling like a walking disaster. I had to realize that my failure was instrumental to who I was, just as the redemption story I was going to embark on. I prayed, leaned into support, and told myself every day one good thing I did to help build my self-love. The small daily steps moved the needle closer to me believing that my past doesn't define me, nor does it dictate what I'm capable of, and doesn't have to be something shameful anymore. I remember during this time of regaining self-love and self-worth was when I became very aware of the content I was consuming and the people I was around. I honed in on calibrating the energy around me. I started listening to my body's responses to daily activities and what I took in. If I got wrapped up in the gossip, or wrapped up in caring about other people's opinions, it took me to a deeper pain. So, I changed the input coming in. I changed the narrative and rewrote the story in loving myself with all my flaws. I am still very intentional with protecting my peace and my self-love bubble.

Part of this healing was also realizing that saying I loved myself wasn't making me selfish. I had grown up thinking you love others first and foremost, and that you are a defender of protection at all costs; that you are a rock for others and make sure everyone knows how much they are valued, even if it cost you falling into pieces. This was the missing magic. I am so glad I learned that to truly love others and to receive their love, you have to love yourself first. It wasn't selfish to take time to pamper myself, or to speak encouragingly and lovingly to myself. This was the utmost respect for others because only then was I able to fully give back.

As my mother told me, you truly do have a choice in life. You can dim your light, your worth, and your purpose, or you can work through your doubts, pains, and character defects to unveil them as some of your strongest attributes. I had to realize that if I was ever going to heal, I had to know I was worthy of love again. I was worthy to know that I could make more of my life. I had to remind myself daily that past mistakes were not all there was to me, and more importantly, that I can help so many others grow from their story. Maybe your story isn't as traumatic, or maybe it's more so, but that's the beauty of it because we all have a story. We are all worthy of love and success, and we all have a unique purpose to shine brightly upon others.

Lessons Learned:

1. I learned that my worthiness didn't come from anyone else but from within myself.
2. I learned the foundation of who I really was through pain, trauma, and vulnerability.
3. I learned that I won't dim myself out of fear of judgment.

Mindset Tips:

1. Your past doesn't define who you are or your destiny.
2. You have the power to change your thoughts, words, and actions to become the best version of yourself.
3. Remember, you are not alone in your journey.

Aha Moments and Self-Reflections

Note your Thoughts

Catherine Huddleston

Catherine Huddleston, M.Ed., is a trainer of both horses and humans, author, speaker, coach, and heartfelt believer in acceptance of self and others. A life-long horsewoman, she facilitates emotional agility and communication workshops in personal growth and corporate formats, utilizing horses and their profound knowledge. *"Ask, Allow, Encourage…"* is one of her core programs supporting an approach to a present state of being, self-acceptance, communication, and co-creation. She believes that the best lessons in life come through experiences and that there is no better teacher than a horse. She brings these lessons to life and empowers her clients to take their unique learning and apply it to enhance daily life. With a diverse career as an entrepreneur, business owner, and team and leadership development facilitator, she has touched hundreds of lives in partnership with horses.

Catherine comes from a family of storytellers where stories were used to entertain and educate. She published her first illustrated book, *"Through the Eyes of a Horse"* in 2022 and hosts the podcast, *"Horses Helping Humans."* A horse lover since childhood, she lives with her horse, Cleo, and two rescue dogs.

Connect with Catherine:

huddleston.catherine1@gmail.com

Chapter 4

Finding Self Love Through the Eyes of a Horse

By Catherine Huddleston

As I write these words from this body, this skin I've been living inside of for over five decades, I feel no older than twenty-six. However, the outside of my body carries the wrinkles and scars of so many days, weeks, and years I have walked this earth. But to me, it seems like a blink of an eye. My father has been gone more than half of my life, but on his eightieth birthday, I asked him what it felt like to be eighty?

He said, "Well, I'll tell ya' I feel the same as I did when I was in my twenties. In my mind, I am the same person, but when I look in the mirror, there is a stranger looking back. It goes by quick; don't take it for granted."

I was in my early twenties when we had that conversation, and I didn't truly understand what he meant. Intellectually I did, but I just hadn't had the life experiences to truly comprehend. Today, I have a vastly different relationship with that conversation. The body I reside in has served me well, and I haven't treated her with the respect she deserves. I used to believe that the best way to depart this life was the adage of sliding into home plate wrinkled and broken, with a smile on my face, laughter in my throat, and destruction all around. I treated my body as a tool and used her hard. In the horse world, people say, "Ride 'em hard and put 'em away wet!" And so, I did just that.

As a youngster, I was fearless. I rode backward or standing in the saddle while galloping across fields. I taught my pony to rear on command and would even dive off him at a gallop, rolling under a wire fence on the regular. I believed I was indestructible with a very busy guardian angel at my side, probably two or three. I carried this mindset well into adulthood, bringing amazing adventures and consequences. I laughed, I loved, I lived boldly, and life sped by while I focused on training horses and people.

The consequence of treating myself in this manner was pain, both physical and emotional. I chose a field of work where men and masculinity are revered, even though more than 70 percent of horse owners are women. The horse industry has been patriarchal, providing added challenges for female trainers, even though we are the majority. This means that to survive in the field, I believed I had to be more masculine in my approach to my career. And thus, the divide deepened, and my valuing of personal feminine traits began to exist increasingly in the shadows. Ironically but not surprisingly, this pushed me further and further from my passion, intuition, and the gifts that made me a great trainer and teacher. Several times in my adult life, I have stopped working in the horse industry to recover from burnout. The truth of that statement is that I had to stop to be able to start feeling emotions again and come back to my authentic self. I have paid the price for allowing this consequence repeatedly. Illness and injury have stopped me in my tracks. But the disease I created in my body from not being authentic, listening to or hearing my intuition, and not fully loving myself has been the most devastating.

Self-love is a complicated topic. As an expert in the field of equine facilitated learning, I cannot easily calculate the number of clients that bump up against the idea of loving themselves. Truthfully, as a coach and mentor, it is my responsibility to walk my talk. Thus, I must not only speak to self-love, but I must also embody self-love. I'm not saying it's been easy. I am, however, saying it has been necessary.

I took on a role with a company and a business partner that elevated my career to a new level. While my partner and I were a phenomenal match as co-facilitators, that was the only place we truly thrived. Our primary focus on how we lived, our belief systems, and even how we communicated was at the opposite ends of the spectrum. We lived a grand experiment of co-creating from such diversity. Unfortunately, I took things beyond what served my own highest good. I experienced severe illness in my years in this environment. I developed colitis, a recurring issue that hospitalized me repeatedly over three years. The stress of focusing primarily on making money to survive was killing me from the inside out. All the years I had spent learning to run programs and facilities, only to have my expertise and knowledge set aside repeatedly for ego-driven, outdated practices, created a "make more money only" mindset. I made a name for myself in modernizing programs and facilities to improve the quality of care, reduce expenses, and improve profitability through common sense animal husbandry and management practices. The difference here was that this approach needed to be embraced but was not. Consequentially, the focus stayed on making more money and for me, that exclusivity in profit focus was detrimental. I thrive on service and servant leadership with a fair exchange. Don't get me wrong, I like having a high quality of life which includes money, but I don't align with money first as my primary motivator. My last hospitalization in this environment drove me to create a momentous lifestyle change, but it was too late.

On my third trip to the emergency room and hospitalization for colitis, I was experiencing stabbing pain in my left abdomen that would double me over and stop me in my tracks. It had become an unbearable way of life. I lived in fear of recurrence and all that entailed. Extreme stabbing pain, fever, and cold sweats; emergency rooms with IV's, needles, tests, and repeating the story and symptoms over and over again; fear and frustration, hospitalization, the hated sensation of morphine drips traversing my body causing me not to care, and potent antibiotics that wreaked havoc on the body while hopefully eliminating the infection. I lay in a hospital bed on the fourth of July, waiting to be discharged and alone in my experience. My partner being unwilling to pick me up from the hospital was, for me, finally, the last straw. That $100 cab ride home and walk up the drive was my make-or-break moment.

This was the moment that led to a need to create change in my life and a conversation with my partner, which then led to a substantial change for the business. Within months, I helped the company relocate from southern California to Missouri; from 10 acres of dirt to 40 acres of pasture with year-round working facilities. I helped find the property, relocated everything from tractors to equipment to horses, and set up vendors and partnerships at the new location. I utilized my skill set which felt good, and reconnected with old friends, but the wheels were already in motion. For every action, there is a consequence, not good or bad, but simply a consequence for our choice, action, or lack thereof.

The relocation from California to Missouri occurred at the end of 2013. By the beginning of 2016, I experienced a consequence and was diagnosed with breast cancer. The circumstances that I had been immersed in were not lost on me. I noticed significant changes in a cyst in late 2015 and sought medical intervention. The result was a lumpectomy with no expectation of anything other than a cyst, as per every medical professional consulted and involved. Even my surgeon said he didn't expect any other outcome and he'd only ever been wrong once in thirty-plus years. Still, everything went to pathology. Honestly, I wasn't too concerned with my health as my focus was on my brother who had been diagnosed with stage four metastasized colon cancer a few months prior. His case was complicated by other incredibly significant health issues, and he entered hospice Christmas 2015. He lived three hours from me at the time, and I spent as many weekends with him and our brother, Jerry, as possible. I threw my lumpectomy surgery into the mix in February and, after a week, went back down to be with my brothers. That was the weekend John passed, and two days later, I was diagnosed with breast cancer.

On the Saturday that John passed, we chose to celebrate his life. We went out for a steak dinner and reminisced about his love of food and all the buffets he insisted we take him to. We laughed and shed a few tears while telling our favorite John stories. We went bar hopping and got really drunk, and I mean really drunk. John had talked about wanting the kind of normalcy we lived; having a driver's license and the freedom it empowered, a personal home, going out for drinks—all the things we take for granted. We couldn't give him those things in his life. His journey required other circumstances and experiences. I remember stories of him being committed to the state hospital and thrown in a padded room where he was hosed down daily, as well as how he perceived each transition from one institution to another as if it were a grade in school. He chose to look at his life through the lens of growth and achievement. He was one of my heroes, my big brother that doted on me until the end. So, I celebrated his life, not knowing that less than 48 hours later, I would be dealing with a cancer diagnosis of my own.

When I look back, I was numb. I didn't experience much except dull, stagnated grief for the loss of my big brother. It took me a while to begin to grieve for myself and my body, and I still do periodically, often when I least expect it. The moment of my diagnosis changed my life forever, and I'm still grasping what that means. More tests, another surgery, and seven weeks of radiation ensued. Several profound things came from my diagnosis and treatment; I was confronted with my own mortality, explored when and where I believed the cancer was activated and began growing, and wrote a book for the child within. All the while, turning to my horses for love, comfort, and learning.

Mortality was a daunting and earth-shattering discovery, and eventual reframe for me. I had lived my life up to that point in ways that simply used my body as a tool. It was a tool for sensing others, a tool for communicating with horses, a tool for enjoying life's pleasures to the fullest, and a tool that I could drive past the point of tolerance with an ego that believed there was value and pride in my ability to push beyond despite pain and injury. Facing my mortality meant looking at my fear of missing out by not being alive, and beginning to look instead at genuinely living each day with purpose. I watched my brother die of cancer and, within hours of that experience, was dealing with that truth and possibility for myself. My surgeon was wrong, the radiologist was wrong, and no one and no test designed to see cancer from the outside recognized the tumor. Only pathology caught it. Before surgery number two, to get clear margins, I did more tests; genetic screening was negative, more scans with contrast were negative, and nothing was showing up. We made treatment decisions based on those tests only to find out through pathology that the second surgery found more cancer, and my margins were clear. Future and frequent mammograms would be needed, and self-exams would be pertinent. Ultimately, I had to learn to live with this truth, as tests could not "see" cancer in me. I continue to wrestle with this knowledge, and this possibility. Could I miss something and experience a similar fate as my beloved brother? Truthfully, his ending was hard to watch and be a part of because it was not pretty. In my darkest tear-filled moments, I had to turn and face my mortality while down on my knees. I peered into my heart, knowing I was not complete in my journey or legacy and chose to live. Somewhere inside, I found a glimmer of hope to live life. I decided to begin to make friends with my body and my cancer. I chose not to go to war with the disease but honor my body, the message, the warning, the consequence, and begin to listen to my consort again. Be gentle and honor her truth. Allow her to rest and recover. After all, none of us truly know how long we have in this life, and the journey can be so much more fulfilling by partnering with ourselves.

Throughout treatment, I was meditating on what I believed activated my cancer. I had completed my genetic testing, knowing that both my mother and grandmother had the same type of breast cancer as I, only diagnosed at a later stage. The genetic testing showed that I was negative. After some very intense exploration, what I landed on, what resonated with me to the bone, was that my choice to stay living an inauthentic life, when every fiber of my being was telling me to go, was the trigger. I chose to stay with my partnership to build and acquire my piece of the pie against my intuition. I decided to place the pursuit of money over my value of service first focus. I chose to fight my own internal compass and path to satisfy a hungry and misguided ego. You see, I am incredibly good at facilitating and working with clients. I enjoyed the praise and accolades and was living in a tug-of-war between my own personal heaven and hell on earth. I remember times that I was ill with colitis and in the hospital. I heard that little voice inside say that it was time to let go, and to make changes for my own highest good. I chose against that little voice, convincing myself that my ego was right. It wasn't until the fourth of July when I heard the voice again that I made that change, and it was too late. The tipping point had already been met and surpassed. The cancer had likely already begun. The consequence can be so subtle, silent, and the accumulation of those little moments where I chose not to course correct got me. I know I activated the cancer; it was the consequence I never expected, but then again, it seldom is.

About halfway through my radiation treatment, I wrote a story for children and the child within. The story is from my inner child to me. In a moment when I was dealing with not only who I was in this new reality, but also how I would deal with and hopefully accept my body; my consort with her new scars and wrinkles that I saw reflected in the mirror. I crafted a story about a little girl named Cindy, who learns how to accept herself through the unconditional love and acceptance of a horse named Gypsy.

I had been looking to the horses as a part of my healing as I always do. What I remembered is similar to what Cindy learned:

"When she got home that night, she told her parents all about her wonderful day. She was so happy and so tired! As Cindy lay in bed that night, she decided, "From this day on, when I look in the mirror, I'm not going to see all the things I don't like about me; the glasses I wear, my funny messy hair, how my feet turn in a little bit, or even my wheelchair.... I'm going to see what Gypsy saw, my heart!" (a passage from my book "Through the Eyes of a Horse").

So now, when I look in the mirror, I look for what I like about myself; the scars and missing flesh on my breast, the wrinkles and crinkles around my eyes, the salt sprinkled throughout my hair, and the extra pounds on my waist and thighs are all the signs I've lived life! I'm still here, repeatedly rising from the ashes and allowing the fire to strengthen and open my heart, albeit reluctantly sometimes. What makes me who I am from the inside out and how my consort carries the beauty of my lifelong artistic endeavors of scars, tattoos, creaks, and wrinkles are representative of truly having lived life! By remembering to love and accept myself for who I am today, I embody the possibility of living through my consort, my amazing body, in a supportive and loving way.

resiliency (noun): *the capacity to recover quickly from difficulties; toughness*

Throughout my life, I have experienced several impactful events; things that people refer to as "me too" experiences, severe injuries, and accidents. I don't think about those moments in my life until I have to put them down on paper, like at the doctor's office. They're just things that have happened to me, not who I am. However, those experiences, those moments in time, are a part of the woven tapestry of my life that make me who I am today; truthfully, I wouldn't change any of them.

When I see myself through a horse's eyes, I see my heart, authenticity, possibility, love, laughter, joy, discipline, work ethic, pain, fire, faltering, rising, and so much more. I see the glory of my life and all the shades and colors of emotions and sensations to come as I continue to embody life. When I stand and embrace self-love, I love myself at every juncture, whether I like myself or not in each moment. If I love myself through each incarnation, I can be the teacher, student, trainer, speaker, author, friend, daughter, aunt, and leader that I need to be. The power to stand up and move forward with my life, and my resilience is intertwined with self-love. I love myself enough to get up. I love myself enough to want to get to the other side of the circumstance. Honestly, I didn't know there was any other choice.

There are bumps in the road we all traverse, but the road keeps going, so I might as well keep following it. For me, self-love has everything to do with acceptance and resiliency. I don't think about those bumps in the road much after I've gotten through them. My curiosity of what's just around the bend always seems to come first. At every juncture of my life, I have looked to the horses. My heart resides with them. I am happiest when with them. When I slip into my riding boots, it's like putting on my suit of authenticity; a coming home, if you will. With each moment of recovery, my need and desire to be with my horses or sit upon their back have been a critical component in my healing. How they model present state of being, herd dynamics, self-care, and connection teaches me daily to be better. I am a better person, friend, partner, teacher, student, mentor, trainer, facilitator, and member of my community when I follow the teachings of the horse. If I can be fifty percent of the human my horse sees, well then, I can be, and will contribute spectacular things and leave this world for the better.

I must always remember to look at myself through the eyes of a horse. The story of Cindy and Gypsy comes from a place of service. Her story offers the opportunity to see herself reflected back in a way that supports self-love and self-acceptance. My wish for every child and child within is to read or hear this story and begin to see themselves through the eyes of a horse.

"Through the Eyes of Horse" written by Catherine Huddleston and illustrated by Payton Kelly is available everywhere.

HORSES TEACH US:

Congruence: When I mask or hide my emotions or feelings, I am being incongruent. I am inauthentic in this state. Authenticity, and alignment with myself, empowers me. To all sentient beings, incongruence equals a threat. Our innate survival drive heightens when we experience incongruence. This can drive us to react instead of respond. Horses are master teachers and interpreters of incongruence.

Connection: A horse alone is a lonely horse. A human living in isolation is a lonely human. We are both made to live in connection and some version of community, not only with others but also with ourselves. We are not simply the brain inside our skull. We experience life through our body in all its glory. Whether it's physical pain, heartbreak, pleasure, excitement, or even depression, it's all embodied. Our emotional state can be felt by others through affect contagion, which means others can catch our feelings, or we can catch theirs. Think of how a yawn, crying, or laughing can expand through a room full of people. Self-awareness and a good relationship with the self empowers our understanding and experiences of connection.

Present state of being: Right here, right now is all we truly have. Horses are masters of being present and model this beautifully. That's not to say they don't know what has occurred in their life; they do. Horses carry learning instead of baggage. Here's an example: The experience and subsequent story of getting a nip from a small dog as a child can get turned into baggage. The retelling of the story can anchor the fear. With each account and embellishment of the story, as an adult, creates a phobia of dogs. The horses would frame the story as something they experienced and go back to grazing. If it happened repeatedly, they would heighten their awareness and preparedness around that specific type of experience when presented with it, but not dwell on or translate that experience to mean all dogs and live in a state of phobia.

If I can embrace these three teachings as taught by the horse, I can live with a higher quality of life. I can be present in my consort and better respond to her feedback about my environment, choices, and options. I get better at this practice every day by being a student of the horse. By practicing, I have become a better co-facilitator with my horse partners and a better partner to my consort. I can make better choices, respond when my intuition and consort whisper, and live more authentically.

Lessons Learned:

1. When I am in alignment with myself, not masking or hiding my truth, I am capable of making decisions and choices that serve my highest good.
2. When I am in alignment with myself, only then can I truly connect with others. I can connect in the healthiest ways by knowing what is mine emotionally to own, and honor what others are feeling without taking it on.
3. Right here right now is truly all we have. Embracing a fully present state of being enables us to become aligned with self and open the door to connection.

Mindset Tips:

1. Congruence empowers me to hear how my authentic self is guiding me.
2. Connection with others can only occur when I am truly connected to myself.
3. I must be in alignment and connected with myself to fully embody every moment of every day.

Aha Moments and Self-Reflections

Note your Thoughts

Charlene Madden

Charlene Madden is an author, women's empowerment coach, Reiki practitioner, and mental health awareness speaker. Charlene candidly shares her experiences of spending most of her life living in a state of darkness. After experiencing over nine years of childhood sexual trauma, over a decade of domestic violence, and 30+ years of mental illness and suicidal ideology, she has been able to step out of that darkness and into the light. Healing her mind, body, and soul led her to a path of purpose, which is working to break down the walls of stigma around child abuse and mental illness, as well as helping others to find their own purpose and live a life of passion. The beautiful mountains of British Columbia are where Charlene calls home and where she shares her little piece of heaven with her husband and their many pets.

Connect with Charlene:

https://www.facebook.com/CharleneAnneMadden
https://www.ascensionwellnessstudio.com
https://www.tiktok.com/@charlenemadden1

Chapter 5

Bulletproof Life

By Charlene Madden

I remember hearing a quote once, I'm not sure who by, but it said, "What if one moment could change your life forever?" I remember thinking about that quote as I turned off the ignition of my SUV in the parking lot of the hotel where the "Life by Design" women's workshop was being held.

Here I was sitting in my vehicle, hesitating to go inside, because I was not at all looking forward to the next two days. I had begrudgingly agreed to attend the event after a co-worker had approached me just two weeks prior. She mentioned to me that it was meant to be an empowerment event for women and asked if I was interested in going with her. Without hesitation, I said "No," because a weekend full of "rah-rah, sis, boom, bah" energy was the last place I wanted to be.

I mustered as much politeness as I could and declined her invitation. She immediately looked disappointed when I declined and said something that would change my life forever: "Please will you come with me? I really want to go but I don't want to go alone."

Damn her. It was almost like she knew my weakness. I hated to see others suffer or be disappointed. It was probably why I had always put everyone else first and stuffed my own needs down at the bottom of the priority list as I had done most of my life.

I gave an internal sigh and gathered up as much energy as I could to slap the fake smile on my face that I knew I was going to have to wear up to and during the event. "Okay, I'll go with you," I responded, and the smile spread across her face. As much as I didn't want to go, I knew deep inside that she needed as much self-empowerment as you could stuff into her. So, it would be a small sacrifice of my time to go.

Now, as I was siting in my car trying to motivate myself to go in, I realized that maybe it was a bigger sacrifice than I thought. It was a sacrifice of time, and that was something that I didn't have much left of. That Saturday was going to mark the last weekend that I was going to spend alive. I had only two days left before the date that I had set to take my own life; did I seriously want to spend it in a room full of strangers pretending that I was okay? Part of me thought it was a great idea. No one would suspect that on Monday morning I was planning on driving up to the mountains and using the gun that laid in the back seat of my SUV to end my pain. No one would think that I was weak, and see the trauma that I had carried for so long had finally become too much to bear. Maybe this was the perfect mask to wear for my last two days.

So, I grabbed my purse, and got out of vehicle, taking a brief moment to ensure that the blanket that laid on the floor covered the rifle and the box of bullets. The last thing I needed was to have to explain why I was driving around with a gun in my backseat. I knew there would be too many questions given what the last few years of my life had entailed.

I ascended the stairs to the conference room, smiled as I was handed my name tag, opened the doors and entered the room full of tables. There it was, that familiar feeling that seemed to bubble up from the pit of my stomach. I'm not sure if you've ever felt it before, but it's that feeling of not belonging. I walked into that room full of beings who, to my eyes, fit the mold of what happy, successful and put together women was supposed to look like, and here I was inside feeling like nothing more than a fraud.

I crossed the room and passed by tables of women who were laughing and talking, excited about the speakers, the plans and goals that they were making for their lives and the upcoming year, and here I was just trying to get through the next two days so that I could end my life. I wondered what they would think about me if they could only read my mind. I'm sure they would be shocked, and probably disgusted, which would be mirroring the thoughts that I carried about myself. Luckily, I had long ago let go of my fear of what people would think about me. I had embraced the feelings that I was always going to be someone who had no value, so of course everyone would think poorly of me, and I needed to get used to it.

I sat down at an almost empty table, put my head down and started to scribble away on the notepad that was included in our gift bag. I knew that if I looked busy or deep in thought that no one would bother me, though in fact, I really was in deep thought. Finally making the decision to end my life had an almost calming effect. It had finally quieted the voices that seemed to be constantly bombarding me with the negative thoughts.

The silence seemed to allow me the space to reflect on my life from the perspective of an observer. I looked at the trauma-filled childhood that I had endured, seeming almost to disassociate from the over nine years of sexual abuse at the hands of my grandfather. I looked sadly at my adolescence and the lack of understanding from anyone in my life who could have made a difference that I needed help to deal with the trauma. I looked lovingly at the coping mechanisms that I had engaged in, even in their dysfunction, knowing that had they not been present, I wouldn't have been able to make it to this point.

I looked back at my failed marriage. I had married my high school sweetheart, hoping and praying that I was going to be able to break the family curse that seemed to follow me. I had hoped that I was going to be able to provide a safe and loving household for my children that I had never known. How though, do you create something that you have never seen? It broke my heart knowing that through my own dysfunction, I had passed on pain and heartache to my children. Still, I smiled thinking about the three amazing children I had been blessed with. They, and they alone, had been the lighthouse in the storm, the anchors that had kept me tied to life, and now they had all grown and moved on and were creating lives of their own.

My mind then went back to the rifle in the backseat of the vehicle that sat down in the parking lot. I remember someone saying that suicide was a cowardly way out, and how angry I felt by that. Obviously that person had never had the barrel of a gun in their mouth trying to desperately muster up the courage to pull the trigger and end their pain. No, suicide wasn't weakness, but it wasn't strength either. It was just a compiling of pain and trauma that finally becomes too much, and you seek a reprieve.

I knew this far better than I should. And so, the last memory slipped forward.

Just two years before, I was starting my life over; I had just ended a thirteen-year relationship, and was heartbroken. I hid as much of the pain as I could from those around me because the ending of the relationship, even though it was painful, was the best thing that could happen for me. The relationship had consisted of nothing but toxicity and dysfunction. There had been domestic violence, alcoholism, adultery, and addiction, and a belief deep inside that everything I was on the receiving end of was exactly what I deserved. How do you believe that you deserve to be loved and cherished when you've never experienced it? Trauma and abuse were all I seemed to know, and it felt almost like home; like someplace comfortable.

Only two short months after the relationship ended, with my partner leaving me for another woman, I was notified that he had committed suicide. He had driven up into the mountains and used his own rifle to end his pain and suffering. His battle was over, and he was no longer charged with having to fight a battle that he didn't have the weapons to face. Deep down I envied his escape, even though I had to bear witness to the pain that was left behind, I yearned for my own peace.

As my table started to fill up with eager attendees, I was forced to leave behind my thoughts, and once again don my mask of normalcy. I watched as all of the ladies settled in and noticed with a little resentment how each table seemed to be filled with a group of ladies that all seemed to know each other, and how it all seemed so cliquey to me. It was just another reminder that I was never going to fit in. The Emcee and Hostess of the event took the stage to kick off the weekend, and with no hesitation, the DJ started to play some music and the first speaker headed to the front of the room to give her talk.

The morning session seemed to creep slowly by. I feigned engagement as best as I could even though I couldn't relate to any of the topics that were being spoken on. I'm sure to everyone else in the room the topics on diet and exercise, and financial health were topics that they wanted to know more about, but for myself as each speaker got on stage, I kept thinking that it didn't matter to me because in two short days I would be dead, so losing weight and saving money really weren't important to me.

The lunch break finally came, and I faked excitement and went off to lunch with a couple of the ladies from my table, including the co-worker who had invited me. I listened with as much attention as I could as they each spoke about what their takeaways had been from the speakers. I was thrilled when the lunch break ended before I had a chance to share my takeaways. I was honestly running out of energy and wasn't sure how believable I could be anymore.

We entered the conference room, the DJ had the music pumping, and several ladies were up dancing. I remember feeling that spark of excitement. Music had always been my lifeline during the dark times; it had been a place to escape to, and for as long as I could remember, I had loved to dance. I remember thinking that if this was going to be one of my last days on earth then screw it, I was going to dance and enjoy myself. So, for just a few brief minutes, I gave into myself. I allowed the joy to flow through me unbridled by all the negative talk. All too quickly though, the music ended, and we were asked to take our seats once again.

I took my seat along with the other ladies at the table and prepared myself for another three hours of unrelatable ramblings by well-meaning individuals. The music started and the Emcee announced the next speaker to the stage. I watched as a woman took the stage that didn't look like any of the other speakers who had come before.

There on the stage in all her bald glory, stood the next speaker. She introduced herself and began to share her story. Her name was Vanessa, and she was here to spread her message of self-love. She spoke of her journey with alopecia, which is an autoimmune disease that causes your body to lose its hair. She spoke of the struggles that she faced as a young child and a young woman. She poured her heart out discussing the pain of not fitting into society's ideal box of what a woman is supposed to be. She talked about not feeling like she fit in and how her struggles with self-love and self-acceptance led her down a path to depression, as well as alcohol and drug use; she spoke about not knowing where she would be right now had she not learned to love herself, to accept herself just as she was, and to set aside the pressures that society put on her regarding beauty. She knew she was enough just as she was, and she wanted other women to know that as well.

I listened intently to her story, feeling a deep connection with her. I knew that deep down inside I had never felt enough. I had never felt accepted by anyone in my life, but more importantly, I had never accepted myself. I remember as she was walking off the stage hearing a small voice in the back of my mind that said, *What about you?* I remember thinking how differently my life could have been had I learned to love myself. If I had learned that I was enough, maybe things would have been different. Just as quickly as that voice had come though, it disappeared once again, but I was left with a strange feeling.

Soon the Emcee was announcing the next speaker and I watched as she made her way to the stage. Her name was Shyloe and she was a teacher, but she was also someone who had lived with and experienced mental health and depression for over 20 years. I once again leaned forward in my seat, curious as to what she would share. She spoke about her struggles and how she had been in the depths of darkness, feeling lost and hopeless. I felt my heart clench as I completely understood her feelings of hopelessness.

But then, she shared a message of hope. She shared how she realized that to live a life worth living she needed to learn to love herself, and that meant loving all of her, including her mental illness. She knew that she needed to accept that part of herself as much as she accepted every other part of herself, and that by accepting and loving the dark parts of herself, it allowed her to pull them into the light, which led her down a path of healing.

As she finished her story and left the stage area, I once again heard that small voice in my mind that said, *What about you?* I sat back in my seat and pondered how differently my life would have been had I learned to live with my mental illness. How differently could my life have been had I learned to love that part of me as well, learned to pull the darkness close and allow the light to shine into it? Once again though, I brushed away those thoughts because my mind had been made up; it was too late to learn how to love myself and it was too late to learn to accept that part as well.

The final speaker was announced and was brought to the stage. There stood a gentleman by the name of Jerrod and he began to share the journey he had been on over the last few years. His journey had taken him through a failed marriage, losing custody of his children, facing addiction to pain medication and alcohol, and living with depression, mental illness and suicidal ideology. I once again leaned forward in my seat thinking how much his story paralleled my life: a failed marriage, walking away from my kids, alcoholism, and being suicidal. I listened as he shared how one moment changed his entire life.

Jerrod had spent the last year trying to find the perfect mix of pain medication and alcohol, which would lead to an overdose. He knew that if he committed suicide and made it look like an accidental overdose, his children would be taken care of through his life insurance, and at the time that was the only value he felt he served of them. So, one evening on a rare occasion where his ex-wife asked him if he could take the kids overnight, he found that perfect mix of pain medication and alcohol. As his children slept, he laid on the couch feeling himself slowly slipping away knowing that this was the moment he had prayed for so long, yet in this moment he heard a small voice that said "No, not like this, not today."

He was able to reach his cell phone and call for help and, in that moment, his entire life changed. He was taken to the hospital where he received medical care and was put on a path to healing. He received help for his mental illness struggles and for his addiction issues, and for the first time in his life, he felt hope. As he went through recovery, he realized part of his healing came through sharing his story and by hopefully helping someone else who may be going through the same struggles as he was at that time.

He finished his talk and walked off the stage to an enormous round of applause, as well as many tear-stained cheeks. His story had impacted so many, but probably none more than me. As I leaned back in my chair, I glimpsed around the room, almost expecting there to be a hidden camera and someone popping out, as if anyone knew what was going on in my mind at that time. Once again, I heard that small voice. *What is going on right now?* The thought repeated over and over in my mind. What were the chances that I was: #1) At an event that I didn't even want to go to, and #2) Had just heard three stories from three different speakers on the areas of my life that I had been struggling so desperately with?

I realized right then and there that it wasn't an accident that I was sitting in that seat. I was exactly where I needed to be at that moment in time. I needed to hear the message that if I loved myself, it was enough, and I didn't need anyone else to validate my worth. I needed to accept myself, the good parts and the bad. More importantly though, I needed to get honest with myself and the people around me. Only *I* was going to be able to save myself and, maybe, just maybe, going on that journey would mean that I could save others as well.

Three simple messages had changed my life: **Self-Love, Self-Acceptance, and Self-Responsibility.**

I crossed the parking lot of the hotel at the end of that night and glanced down at the rifle laying under the blanked in the backseat. Everything was going to be different now because I knew that the person who stood beside that car wasn't the same person who had stood beside it earlier that day. No, this person had hope for the life that lay ahead, and a newfound purpose.

This began my journey of evolution and growth; a journey that started with making hard decisions, looking fear in the eyes, and getting honest with myself and everyone around me. I spent the next week making plans to create the changes that I knew I deserved to make. I reached out to a close friend, who, without any questions, agreed to take all of the firearms in my house. I spoke to my boss about holding my pain medication, and I started to have conversations with those closest to me about how I had been struggling. I knew that in order change, I was going to have to pull off the Band-Aids that I had been using to cover my wounds.

The most important conversation that I had, though, was with myself. I was no longer going to allow fear to control my life. I could no longer sit in the shadows; I needed to rise out of the ashes and blaze like the phoenix that I knew was buried within.

I looked at all of the things I had allowed fear stop me from doing. I made a choice to publish the book of poetry that I had started writing in high school. All of those words that I had poured out as a survival mechanism were a compilation of all of the pain and heartache that I had experienced over my life. If I was going to get honest, it meant I had to share all of the parts of myself.

I challenged myself to ask someone out on a date. This choice was not made because I wanted to be with someone—for the first time in my life, I was okay with the thought of being alone—rather it was because I wanted to prove to myself that even if I faced rejection, I was still going to be okay. Much to my surprise, the person I asked out agreed, and I am happy to say that nine months after our first date we were married.

I had also made the decision that I wanted to take my story, my struggles, and all of the pain and heartache that I had experienced, and use it for good. I made the choice to start sharing my story publicly in hopes that someone would be able to be gifted hope, just as I was that day.

The following year, I went back and spoke for the very first time at that same event that had changed my life. I shared my story knowing that someone sitting in that audience could be feeling the exact same way I was just a year prior.

When I finished my talk and was heading to the back of the room to join the other speakers, a woman who had been in the audience approached me. She said "Charlene, you know how during your talk you said that if just one person could hear your story and their life be saved, everything you went through would be worth it? Well, I just want you to know that today you saved a life." She then turned and walked away. I remember standing there, more than a little shocked, and then I heard that familiar little voice, the one that I had finally learned to listen to, and it said "Okay, then let's go find one more!"

I have had the opportunity to speak at other events; I have spoken on over 65 podcasts in the past year, and I created and ran my own workshop entitled, "Ignite Your Life" as a way of bringing inspirational women together to share stories of survival, resilience, and power. Through stepping into my own growth and healing, I was led to start my own wellness business called Ascension Wellness Studio, where I offer services meant to assist in the healing of mind, body and soul through Reiki and Transformational Coaching services.

Today, the life I live is a life searching for that one more person who needs to know that they are worth it. They have the power to incorporate self-love, self-acceptance and self-responsibility into their own lives so they, too, can create a life of passion and purpose.

Three Lessons Learned – The 3 S's

1. Self-Love: The moment that you are able to stop searching for outside validation and instead turn your focus inward and learn that to love yourself is the greatest gift, and the first step to creating the life of your dreams. To know that self-love is enough, opens the door to true happiness.

2. Self-Acceptance: When we come to the realization that we can't change the past, we can't change what happened to us or the choices that we made, we move into a state of acceptance. To be able to accept who you are in this moment, the good, the bad and the ugly, with the knowledge that acceptance doesn't mean you can't change, is the second step to creating the life you desire.

3. Self-Responsibility: One of the hardest things you can do in your life is to embrace self-responsibility. When you are able to understand that the choices you make now are your responsibility, regardless of the pain or trauma that created the decisions of your past, you now have the ability to make different choices, and that is powerful!

Mindset Tips

1. You cannot reach for anything new while you hold onto the clutter of the past. You have the choice to release the past and move forward to a happier and healthier life, or you can continue to cling to that which does not serve you.

2. If you want to have something you've never had, you're going to have to do something you've never done. We cannot create the lives we desire using the same thinking that got us to this point. If you want something different, you have to do something different. Find out what that looks like and do it.

3. If cauliflower can become pizza, you, my friend, can become anything. Don't let anyone, including yourself, tell you who or what you have to be. You have the ability to recreate yourself and become the person you've always wanted to be; all it takes is courage and faith.

Aha Moments and Self-Reflections

Note your Thoughts

Helena Smolock

Helena Smolock, is an award-winning CPT-RNC, a Master Athlete, and the Founder and President of Velocity Athletic Training. She received the Business Excellence Award from the Langley Chamber of Commerce in 2003, was voted by clients and business associates across Canada and the USA as Business Person of the Year (2020-2022), seated at #4 in the top ten businesses in the USA, seated at #1 as Business Person of the Year in Blaine, WA, and seated at #6 in the top ten Business People of the Year 2023 in the USA. She has been a Fitness Columnist for *Canadian HealthStyle Magazine*, and *The Langley Times,* and has been featured on radio and television.

From athletes and corporate professionals to those seeking post-rehab, Helena has provided an environment where a trusted bond is developed between client and coach. After many years of self-discovery and praying for "Mr. Right," Helena now resides in Blaine, WA, and is happily married to an amazing man. They enjoy taking their dog for a stroll along the beautiful beaches in and around Blaine and across the border from British Columbia, Canada.

Connect with Helena:

https://instagram.com/@velocityrocks
Helena Smolock CPT-RNC, Master Athlete | LinkedIn

Chapter 6

What's Self Love Got to do with It?

By Helena Smolock

It is a simple craving, much like chocolate, but at times comes with so many complexities— LOVE, the most talked about, shared, and experienced emotion in the entire world!

Yet, so many people never experience its beauty.

I've had quite a journey in experiencing love—well, at least what I thought was love. I've failed at it twice in my life. Though, perhaps I need to ask myself if LOVE has failed me? What I thought was going to be forever the first time around only brought me heartache; a scar that not even a Band-Aid could stop the bleeding. What had I done wrong? Was it me? Was it him? Who knows? It ended as quickly as it started, and through the intricate web of deceit, many got emotionally hurt. These are the complexities of humanity; we can run more than a mile while exercising because we love ourselves, and we nurture ourselves through self-care, but we often can run much further away from loving someone else, not fully understanding why we are running away from them.

Maybe we are running away from mirrors of ourselves… What's self-love got to do with it?

Self-love is learned between the ages of 0-5 years old. We learn from those who guide us, our very own first responders—our parents. While many children in this world experience abandonment, there are others who do not experience a full abandonment, with both parents present, yet a child can still feel alone. When there is no real guidance or nurturing, little attention is given to shape and transform a child into what their true purpose in life is.

I was the latter child. I was born and raised in Ottawa, Ontario, Canada, and was the eldest of what started off as myself and my two sisters, but the clan grew to five children when my mother found out she was pregnant later in life; I was 16 years old. While everyone around me was happy for her and my father, I felt otherwise.

Why?

My parents owned restaurants, which meant they had little time to spend with their three daughters. So, at the age of 10 years old, I was designated as mother, dad, and eldest sister to my two sisters. Not only did I play those roles, but I had the responsibilities of an adult, which meant that once my parents left the house at 6 a.m., I was the one to wake up my sisters, make us breakfast, get us ready for school, and off we went together. Lunch time would come around and we would walk home together (thankfully, the school was down the street from our home), have lunch, and head back to school for the afternoon. School would end, and together we would return home where my responsibilities were grand.

Once we were inside the house, I would wait for a phone call from my mother. We had an established code for when the phone would ring. The code was, when the phone rang twice and stopped, that was her calling me. I would then call her back at the restaurant. I was always happy to speak with my parents; it felt like a normal relationship with them and it was a trusted one. For them, it was knowing that I was being responsible, ensuring that we were in the house, and no friends were allowed over while they were not home. We were not allowed to answer the front door if someone knocked or rang the doorbell. My mother always explained that for safety reasons, it is best that we were safe alone in the house.

It sure felt safe. I had developed a system for myself and my sisters; a schedule when we went to school and returned home. While at home, we each had a responsibility, which included cleaning; I did all the cooking, being the eldest, because I felt it necessary not to have my younger sisters touch a stove. At the end of our responsibilities, we would sit together and do homework.

On some days, my father would surprise us on our way back home from school, and he would be waiting to pick us up to drive us to our grandparents' home. It was my happiest time, knowing that we were heading to see grandma and grandpa! I loved my grandparents. Spending time with them was always fun and I felt freed from my responsibilities. I felt I can be a normal child, enjoying my childhood years without the worries of cooking, cleaning, and ensuring that there were no strangers knocking at our front door.

By the age of 14, I had grown up and matured much quicker than my friends. I had no idea of the concept of self-love as I had been providing love, and guiding my parents, my sisters, my friends, and extended family members. Most often, I felt alone, and at times when I needed the love and nurturing, no one was there and if they were, it was only to take from me. Was I grasping the concept of self-love? Not at all. I continued to get knocked out by people I thought were my friends, who I thought loved me, and who I thought I could trust.

At the age of 16 years old, my perception of self-love was distorted when a handsome Italian man noticed me. His words touched me, he was sweet, exceptionally good looking, and wanted to marry me! He was four years older than I was, but our age difference did not matter; what mattered was the longing to be together, to love and hold one another. He wanted to follow the cultural respect of asking my father for my hand, which scared the heck out of me. I refused to allow that to happen. I was too young and knew exactly what my father's response would be to him as he had not been the only man knocking on my father's door to ask the same question: "Can I marry your daughter?"

I kept this relationship a secret, and it felt safe. Someone was there to love me and nurture me; someone I trusted. I did not want anything to disrupt it. I did not want anyone to break us. Until one day, his behaviour changed overnight. It was like a bad rainstorm had come in with loud thunder; sharp crackling sounds came through his voice when he told me that he had decided to move on because he had a pregnant girlfriend. I had no idea about the girlfriend. I thought I was his one and only. I had no one to turn to or tell the story to; no one to share my pain and loss with. He was my first love; a knight in shining armour, and someone I thought was with me forever.

Once again, I had not thought about myself in the long term. The emotion of love took over me, and embraced my heart completely. I was taken aback by the amount of attention I had received from this man whom I thought was the most handsome man in the world!

I had asked myself many questions—What did I do wrong? How could I overlook this? What did I not see? Was I not enough for him? Was she more beautiful than I? Did she have a better body?

My perception of love had been shattered! What's self-love got to do with it?

As time passed, the wound started to close and eventually healed as I moved on into my early 20's. I felt by then, I had accomplished much more than my circle of friends had. It was evident in our behaviour, thought patterns, and emotional patterns. I am a highly emotional individual with a high sensitivity vibration. It is easy for me to feel and read everything about a person, and at times, I shut it down as it can be too much. I have learned now at the age of 58, to not shut it down but to honour it and listen to that inner voice that says NO. Simple, straight-out NO.

In 1983, in my hometown Ottawa, there was an exceptionally large Lebanese community. It was a vibrant community; I do not think I ever had a dull moment going to parties where I enjoyed belly dancing and a dance called the Dabke. Those were great times that are now wonderful memories to reflect upon. It was at one of those parties where I met a man who asked me to dance. We embraced one another and every so often through the dance, we would share a few words. When the dance was over, he thanked me, and we went our separate ways. Never in my thoughts did I imagine that he and I would get set up by a friend of mine to date one another.

For identity purposes, I will refer to him as M. We started dating, which quickly resulted in an engagement due to the demands of my dad. Culture was the motive to get engaged as it was improper for his daughter to be out and about dating, and dare if any family members saw me with M. I like to think of gossip as lighting a match and throwing it into a haystack, and how quickly that haystack burns up is exactly the way gossip would spread in our community.

On July 26th, 1986, M and I got married after a few months of being engaged. We thought, or should I say I thought, this would be my forever. We've all heard of the signs that the universe gives us, little signals to wake us up, and shake us a bit to listen to that inner voice that says NO. Well, I ignored my inner NO. It rained on the day of my wedding, and the ceremony was being held outdoors at Stanley Park in Ottawa, which had a huge gazebo and a beautiful view.

The park overlooks the Ottawa River and has a view of Quebec as well. The ceremony was set for 3 p.m. Thoughts raced through my head as it rained, as well as the talk my dad had with me a month prior to the wedding, asking me, "Are you sure about this guy?" My response was, "Dad, I love him." We have so much to learn about love; when the wise speak to us, we tend to ignore their messages, and we tend to believe what our youthful heart tells us, believing in it, and believing it is the truth.

By 2:30 p.m., the rain had finally stopped. Friends and family were at my house, the bridesmaids were ready, I was ready to head out in a Cadillac, my father was with me in the car, and the groom's best friend drove the car. The bridesmaids had left in another vehicle. The groom's best friend drove the scenic route, along the Ottawa Parkway to Wellington Street. As we sat at a stop light on Wellington Street, I looked over at my dad, and he had his head down, almost looking sad. I kept silent. Beside us was a car with a man honking his horn at me, yelling at me to roll down the window, so I did. He yelled out, "No, don't do it! Turn around. Date me! You are so beautiful!" I smiled and said, "Thank you." My father finally looked up at me and said, "We can turn the car around," and the groom's best friend added in his comment, "I can turn it around right now!" I commented, "Oh my goodness, really!? This is unbelievable. We are almost there! Isn't anyone happy for me?" They looked at me and begrudgingly agreed that they should be happy for me. We arrived at the ceremony. It was beautiful, and had warmed up quickly. I walked down the aisle, and we said our vows.

The marriage lasted five years, and we had a beautiful son, however, near the end we fought. My husband had deceived me when I found out he was putting ads in the local paper to meet others at swing parties. This was something I found out by chance when I found nude photos of men and women in his sock drawer. It explained the weekends away, supposedly with his friends.

Remember how the word NO was the first word that came out of a stranger's mouth on my wedding day? It wasn't until years later, when I told the story to someone who has strong faith in Christ, that I realized what the message was. He commented, "My dear Helena, God was speaking to you through those men, and you did not listen." I agreed; I did not listen. A warning was thrown in my face and I ignored the sign, and the message being sent to me.

Shortly after the divorce, I headed to British Columbia, Canada, where I knew only one person. I wanted to free myself so I flew the nest. I thought about my life and how much I had done for so many people, which included friends and my family.

I boarded a Greyhound bus in Ottawa on July 1st, 1994, and took my trip across Canada to travel to the great west! What a journey that was! I had never been away from my immediate family, and some of my friends even made a bet that I would be back to Ottawa in a heartbeat.

My travel from province to province was exciting! Not only did I see our beautiful country, but I also had the greatest opportunity to meet fellow Canadians traveling to their various destinations. What I remember most about my journey across Canada was that I had fallen asleep, and when I woke up and looked out the window, the most beautiful scenery was right before my eyes! We had entered Banff, Alberta, and I stared in awe at the mountains, the colour of the water, and waterfalls trailing down from some of the highest mountains I had ever seen. My eyes started tearing because the beauty made me feel so close to God. I looked at the person next to me and asked him, "Do you feel God?" He looked at me strange, but I realized how spiritually evolved I am compared to most people, including my friends. Anytime I did mention God to my friends, they would tell me I was weird. Later in life as I evolved, I learned that I was an Indigo child. These are children who see, hear, and feel empathy at a very high vibration. It explained why I would always cry for my friends. I believed later in life that my crying for them was me wanting to help them and save them.

On July 3rd, I arrived in Coquitlam, British Columbia, Canada at 11 p.m. It was a long trip and I was happy to finally arrive to my new home. As I stepped off the Greyhound bus, I stood for a while absorbing the newness; the air had a different smell, and the environment seemed heavier. What I was sensing was so much First Nation history. It was quite strong, and despite the busy city life, there was still a history of the ancient lingering around. My friend gave me a big hug and welcomed me to B.C. I was so exhausted from three days of taking the bus across Canada, that I needed a good night's rest on a mattress!

The next morning, my friend and I headed out to Vancouver. I wanted to let go of what I left behind, and to begin experiencing what my new life in a new province would be. We took the city bus, which was great because I got to see more of the city as we headed out of Coquitlam. We came to a station, and I felt like a little kid in some sort of fair when we boarded the Skytrain! The city amazed me—the mountains, the warmth and vibe of the city—all of it felt so new and exciting! We finally arrived at Granville station and it was so different than Ottawa.

From Granville Station, we took a stroll along Robson Street, had lunch, then headed back to Coquitlam. I had so much going through my mind about this new journey, in a city I was not familiar with. I had no roots, no friends I had grown up with, no family members, and no job. I walked away from everything when I left Ottawa.

I decided to stay positive and create a game plan. My first step was to begin looking for work. I had been working with the Royal Bank in Ottawa and had left after having my son, so I decided to apply at the processing centre in Vancouver. More than a week after applying, I was offered a position. I was excited to land a position with the Royal Bank, and it solidified my internal feelings that moving to British Columbia was going to work out.

I still had the inner voice speaking to me, wondering if this move would work out. I had to prepare for a year to have things put together, such as a place and a job, but I wondered if Vancouver was the city for me. If you recall earlier, I went through a divorce and had a child with my ex-husband. I did not want to continue living in Ottawa, where everywhere I went, I was reminded of a man that betrayed my trust, friends who betrayed me, as well as my own family members who never supported me. It was a taboo to go through a divorce in our family. Cultural beliefs and morals dictate that women are to stay with their husbands no matter the situation, even in an environment where there is domestic violence. I am not that woman.

My ex-husband and I made our divorce comfortable—no bickering, no fighting over the house, which I had the mortgage to, and especially no fighting over our son. We had amicably agreed that I would move to Vancouver, try it for a year, get set up, and if I did want to stay there, I would be ready for when my son would move to live with me. My son came to visit during my first summer in Vancouver. We had fun! He loved the water parks, Granville Island, and the Pacific National Exhibition (PNE). During the year, he also visited at Christmas and March break, and by the summer, he was ready to move to

Vancouver to live with me. I had decided to make British Columbia my home.

By June of 1995, I had a great place in Marpole, where my son and I would live for the next three years. During that time, I focused on myself and my son. We grew in a different way together; it is difficult for children to understand separation and living with only one parent. I had to play the many roles that comes with single parenting... the very same roles that I had as a 10-year-old girl being the mom and dad, yet the difference is this time I had a full- time job.

This phase in my life taught me so much about myself and what I can say NO to. Breaking away from family, friends, and cultural beliefs made me a stronger woman. Today, I love myself even more. After not visiting Ottawa for nearly 20 years, I decided to go pay a visit to the city where I was born and raised.

I learned one thing—no one has changed. Upon arriving at the airport in Ottawa, it felt like I entered a time capsule, one that I went through on every level, not just time, which included emotional, mental and physical. Emotionally, I had allowed myself to go through a healing process of self-identity. Who am I? A question that repeated itself in my mind.

Exploring yourself is exploring self-love, as mentioned in my journey—*What's self-love got to do with it?* I looked in the mirror and saw my mother and my father, their resemblance and physiologically; I have their DNA, and I have the culture within me as well.

Did that all resonate with me when I left? Some of it did. I accepted that I am my parent's daughter; that I am Canadian and I'm plugged in to an amazing culture. I dealt with the emotional aspect through meeting various individuals in

Vancouver, a city that is known for its many practitioners who specialize in healing. I spent time understanding that my very own self-identity was mine and not that of my parents. My parents carried the traditions of what was practiced in what they would refer as "The Old Country," which was Lebanon, a place where in villages the community was strong as were the morals and values that everyone abided by. My self-identity could not align with the thought patterns that were preached to me. Why did I have to get engaged? Why could I not have just dated the very man who fooled around behind my back?

Being the eldest, I had to set the example of those thought patterns, and by the time I reached my teen years, I realized that I was in a box. I couldn't leave home at the age of 14 because the world at that age is a scary place. How would I survive? Where would I live? Visiting Ottawa for the first time in 20 years, I left behind a closed box; one that I opened up in Vancouver and discovered my self-identity and my self-love. I am compassionate, loving, friendly, happy, and athletic. I enjoy meeting others and learning about them. My spirit loves to soar. I've become much closer to God. I developed a solid relationship with Him and learned that at any time I needed anything, all I need to do is ask for guidance, and for answers.

After 20 years of not seeing family and friends in Ottawa, they were still questioning my divorce!? Their thought patterns have never changed, and they never left the nest. I listened most of the time to their stories because they wanted to catch up with me. I heard nothing new; it was the same gossip, the same "in the box" attitude that everyone was in. I felt sorry for them for they have not experienced the world like I have, they did not want to leave and explore the world and its many adventures! Places, people and situations taught me self-love and to honor myself, which has led me to being happy, peaceful, and most importantly, strong.

Three very important lessons learned during my journey to self-love:

1. Be honest with yourself and with others.
2. Learn to step away and take a long, hard look at who you are.
3. Pat yourself on the back for being strong.

My mindset is obviously different than my family. Three things I discovered were:

1. My mind is very creative and I can come up with very original ideas.
2. Being focused and highly organized by putting everything into compartments to access later on, if I need to access them, has served me well. I also have a photographic memory; I take photos in my mind of situations and people and put them into compartments. I believe this stems from having to always be on guard for myself and my sisters.
3. I enjoy my quiet. I enjoy my peace.

Aha Moments and Self-Reflections

Note your Thoughts

Jacqueline Lagrandeur

Jacqueline Lagrandeur is a powerful force for transformation! She is a compassionate, intuitive, Holistic Energy Healer and Hypnotherapist who believes real, long-lasting *change* is an inside job! Jacqueline's own journey of self-development and self-love began over 25 years ago when she first was introduced to Bob Proctor's world-class teachings. Her extensive training, work-life balance experiences, incredible mindset discoveries, and healing transformations fueled her passion for helping others to BE the change they wish to see! Today, she loves to empower and support women in their journey to self-healing and self-love using powerful effective tools and processes for aligning hearts and minds to the frequency of LOVE. Jacqueline is a loving, family-centered mom and wife who enjoys reading inspirational books, listening to classical music, and staying healthy and active.

Connect with Jacqueline:

https://linktr.ee/jacquelinelagrandeur

Chapter 7

A Return to Me: My Healing Journey

By Jacqueline Lagrandeur

Have you ever felt like there must be something ***more*** for your life but you just didn't know what or how to access it? Have you ever felt an internal nudge or desire to BE or DO something different with your life, but you told yourself, "Nah... I can't do ***that***, I'm not (fill in the blank) enough."

If this sounds like you, then my hope is that my story will awaken and inspire you to unlock the greatness within you, so that you may consciously choose the life of your dreams!

It's a return to me, was the soft but clear message I received this time as I questioned myself about my current life situation. I sit back now and smile when I hear these powerful internal messages coming through more easily and frequently than ever. Over the years, I have learned to trust these as my guidance system, my "Grandeur Soul," the All-Knowing or All-That-Is looking out for my best interest and highest good. I believe we all have this gift of "inner knowingness," but we were taught, unfortunately, to seek answers outside ourselves. I am especially grateful for the comfort and peace I feel every day knowing my journey is being guided and supported by something greater than myself; knowing that God or the Universe has my back, and that life is always working ***for*** me, not against me. Loving and trusting the flow of life is everything to me now! What a wonderful place to be! And this is my wish for you!

Have I always heeded my inner voice or paid attention to what the Universe was telling me? Nope! In fact, I didn't trust myself and I was full of self-doubt in the beginning. When I look back on my life now, I realize all those difficult times I endured were pivotal moments pointing me back to my path to self-love and appreciation. My healing journey has been, and I imagine will continue to be, an ongoing process gifting me with invaluable lessons and insight along the way, and I am pleased to share some of my most transformational moments to empower and support you in your own journey to self-healing and self-love.

There have been ample hardships and impactful moments in my life, and over the years, I have become a master of change. With each challenge, I began to notice a pattern; I would live my life honestly, always doing my best, and somehow, unbeknownst to me, I would start to lose myself. Most times, I would become discouraged, disappointed, sad or unhappy. I would then take a hard look at my painful situation and start to ask myself some profound questions. With each unremitting challenge, I knew I wanted better, but I didn't know how to access it. I would then make prayerful requests, be open to guidance from high sources, such as books or other resources, and then ideas or internal messages would come to me that revealed how best to handle each situation. This was when I would find the courage to do the hard work and hope for the best. Was it always the outcome I wanted? Nope! But in retrospect, each challenge enabled me to develop a new perspective, increase my self-esteem just a little more, and unknowingly point to a "return to me." As trying as those times were, they presented valuable information for my growth, deeper self-healing, and increased self-respect and self-love.

Once again, was it easy? Heck no! It was really hard, but I now realize that every step of the way, I was going against what I was taught as a child, which was to give and not receive; to be respectful to others and not be selfish; to be seen and not heard;

to self-sacrifice by making everyone else a priority. I learned to be last and accept this as my truth. Learning to let go of who I thought I was and gradually regaining my personal power was the most challenging part, but ultimately worth every battle won! Little did I know just how much inner strength and resilience I had within me! If only I had learned to trust my soul's wisdom sooner instead of society's expectations; what other possibilities could I have experienced? As a child, I was immensely shy. I was always the last to be picked for games or teams at school, I was bullied, and I had very low self-esteem, confidence, and self-love. These deep wounds of feeling undeserving and unloved were without a doubt painful, but as mentioned, every challenge and hardship throughout my life presented an opportunity to practice my "return to me" muscle! The ME that matters to me; the ME that is deserving; the ME that is seen and heard; the ME that is respectful and loving to myself; the ME that makes wise decisions; the ME that is love and deserving of love. A "return to me" really means a return to who I AM, which is LOVE, to myself and others.

Throughout the years, I have been blessed to learn that the secret to peace, happiness and freedom is the journey from the inside-out, not the outside in—and that means it starts with you. Your best life starts with trusting yourself and tapping into that All-Knowing place inside of you because it holds all the answers you seek for ultimate health, happiness and freedom!

I have gotten much better at loving myself and making myself a priority over the last 16 years, but my journey of self-discovery first began in 1991 when I became aware of a repeated thought loop that said, "There must be something ***more*** for my life than this." I was desperately seeking a better way to live, but I just didn't know what or how to access it! I was a young 25-year-old mom with 2-year-old twin daughters and a husband who was also keen for change. We were just getting started in life and already our routine was a daily grind with minimal pay. We both shared a passion for doing more, and the idea of raising our family in a small mining town, the town we both grew up in with limited job opportunities, were both disheartening and alarming to us, so we began our search for something better! It wasn't long after that a friend introduced us to Bob Proctor's teachings. Bob is a world-class motivational speaker and mentor. I am in such gratitude for learning his concepts and ideas early in life! In a short while, I began to get really excited about the possibility of change in my life based on his exceptional programs. One day, I chose to do something so daring; something that no one I knew in my environment would ever comprehend doing and would require paying a large sum of money to fly out of the country to attend Bob Proctor's one-week long seminar called "The Million Dollar Forum." It was outrageous for us to even consider this as we had no money for such a trip! But with our friend's testimonial and my husband's encouragement, we committed to finding the money and attend this seminar separately, so that one of us could stay and care for the children. Little did I know this experience would entirely change my life! My own seminar experience was at the Ritz Carlton Hotel in Orlando, Florida, where I enjoyed a life of luxury for an entire week. At the event, top international speakers, such as Jack Canfield, Mark Victor Hansen and Bob, himself, shared their inspiring stories and presented concepts and ideas I hadn't heard before. I will always treasure this incredible life experience, which confirmed to me that there really was much more to life than I had imagined, and it was available to me if I chose it! My greatest learning from this experience was that the power of desire, attitude, and action could make anything happen, and together, they would create a powerful combination to realize my wildest dreams! I began to use his ideas and concepts immediately. Without question, this was the most awe-inspiring adventure I had ever experienced, and it significantly changed the trajectory of my life!

Before returning home, however, I will never forget the "crabs in the bucket" analogy that Bob shared; it signaled that the people back home would have little understanding of these new concepts and my life's ambitions, and they unconsciously would want to pull me back down into "normality." I heeded his warning, and the struggle was real. For many years thereafter, I continued to live between two very conflicting worlds: One defined by hopes, dreams and possibilities, which I later understood grew from conscious intentions, as well as another of problems and misfortunes shaped by subconscious influences.

In 1997, after a long period of struggle in and around Sudbury, Ontario, we made a bold move to uproot our family and relocate to Calgary, Alberta. Despite struggling financially, in a state of what seemed like "survival mode" for years—never seeming able to escape that hamster wheel—with three daughters in tow, it was time for something new. Although the change in our surroundings initially improved our lives, eventually it revealed how much we had been struggling with our marriage. A heavy weight of financial difficulties, combined with long-term instability, produced constant arguments, frustration, and sadness that spiraled into inconsolable disappointment in 2005. The weight I had been carrying for so many years was now crushing me.

Have you ever experienced a time in your life when you felt you gave it your all, but you still came up short? Well, that is exactly how I felt. I was so exhausted with my life, and I had finally come to the realization that there was nothing more for us in our relationship. In fact, we had become more like roommates for many years. It seemed everywhere I went even complete strangers on the street would pick up on my deep sadness without having said a word, and I soon realized my outer shell mirrored the deep sadness I felt inside. Indeed, I was very unhappy and I couldn't hide it anymore, not even from myself. I had lost my way and lost my self. I didn't know who I was, how to feel better, and I didn't know what to do about it. I acknowledged the mess I was in and recognized that I had completely given my power away in this relationship. How did I get here? Where did I go wrong? I started to ask myself important questions and began to consider a new life without my husband. The guilt and shame of possible separation started to consume me. This choice would greatly affect my daughters and tear our family apart. Should I stay for the sake of the children? If so, how much longer? I had invested 18 years of my life already. What example would I be for my girls if I continued to live this way and not be true to myself? I needed to face my reality and started to grieve the inevitable process of divorce. I didn't know what to do and started asking God or the Universe to help me through this immense pain and suffering. The guilt and sorrow were unbearable; I was dying inside... until one night, a miracle happened. I was in my bathroom getting ready for bed when my feelings of sadness began to bubble up again. The pain was so intense that I burst into tears, dropped to the floor and wept uncontrollably while thinking: *What am I going to do? I can't live like this anymore!!* Then all of a sudden, I heard a gentle, yet powerful clear voice. It was so shockingly clear to me, as if someone had been standing right next to me and whispered in my ear. I immediately gasped, stopped crying, and listened. What I heard was, "Jacqueline, if you want your life to ***change***, it's up to ***you***; only you can make the change, no one else." And then as if by magic, a sense of heavenly peace and tranquility washed over me from head to toe as I lay there on the bathroom floor. I remained still, trying to comprehend what had just happened and then I heard it again, "Jacqueline, go to bed now, everything will be ok." This profound message gave me strength and hope for new possibilities ahead. And from that moment on, I knew exactly what I needed to do. I picked myself up off the floor, wiped my tears, and went to bed. For the first time in years, I slept soundly that night. Although I knew I had a lot of work ahead of me, for the very first time in my life, I finally understood that I needed to take full responsibility for my ***own*** life! If it had to be, it was to be ***me***.

You see, up until then, I had endured a lot of suffering and unconsciously allowed myself to be pulled in directions that I had never really wanted. I recognized this "suffering" was of my own unconscious choosing and I had placed my life and my happiness in someone else's hands! That night, I was divinely inspired to finally put a stop to my self-inflicted misery and started taking my life into my own hands. I finally understood nobody else was "going to save me," which was clearly a subconscious belief I had been holding onto all those years. Making new choices for ***my*** life and my children was my path forward, and so I did!

Now, I know some of you reading this might be feeling overwhelmed and discouraged. Some of you might be feeling defeated; tired of working so hard, tired of the responsibilities that you have at home, and with your children. You may feel overwhelmed with the countless to-do lists, and perhaps feel trapped, wishing and hoping that things will change. I'm here to tell you that I never understood the value of my ***own*** power until I started to quiet myself and truly listen to the messages I was receiving. I believe we all receive internal messages, but the question is, are we quieting ourselves enough to listen? Equally, <u>never</u> forget that YOU have choices! Each day is an opportunity to decide how to shape your life, no matter what obstacles come your way. You don't need anyone else's permission or approval; it starts with YOU and making the decision to take action!

Once I chose to take full responsibility for my ***own*** life and my daughters' lives, new ways seemed to magically open up for me!! Was it scary? Hell, yes! I was heading into the unknown, but curiously, I also felt a new energy coursing through me as if something powerful within had set me free! With this new decision, I found the courage within and trusted that everything was going to be ok. Did I know all the steps? Nope! All I knew was that I had to make a different choice, commit to my decision, and take the first step. Just as I did back in 1991, trusting my decision and choosing to believe all would be ok on my new path was my Saving Grace!

For over 25 years, I had worked in a medical environment enjoying many roles, but the one I loved the most was as a medical transcriptionist. After hearing the countless stories and experiences first-hand from dictating physicians and specialists, in 2007, I began to feel a calling toward learning alternative methods and more natural ways of treating and healing. In my view, conventional western medical practices seemed to only mask problems, not find the root cause or treat the whole person, and I wanted to make a difference. It was at this time that I began my next season of self-development. The first course I completed was Feng Shui, where I learned how to improve the energy in my home environment to support all areas of my life. Thereafter, due to my profound curiosity with the power of the mind and the healing arts, I chose to delve deep into Hypnosis and Hypnotherapy. Learning about the conscious and subconscious mind, plus experiencing my own breakthroughs and healing with hypnotherapy inspired me to start my own practice as a Certified Hypnotherapist. In my practice, I helped my clients reprogram their limiting beliefs, release patterns of self-sabotage, and empowered them to transform their lives. I cannot even begin to fully describe the deep transformations experienced personally and by my clients using Hypnotherapy! It was a catalyst for my changed life and long-lasting results, including a personal sustained weight loss of 50 pounds. Additionally, I learned and studied Neurolinguistic programming, Emotional Freedom Technique, Psych-K and Spring Forest Qigong. I also became a certified Holistic Reflexologist, Usui Reiki Master, Certified Coach Practitioner, and Stress Management Consultant. Over the last

16 years, with each healing modality, I continued to experience and embrace increased self-awareness, personal growth and passionately shared these amazing tools and techniques with my clients in my part-time healing practice.

In late 2013, after many years as an overworked full-time medical transcriptionist and part-time health and wellness entrepreneur, I realized just how much my life was out of balance. All that focus on personal and financial achievement had left me feeling exhausted again and questioning my purpose. *Where is my joy?* A new energy was emerging in my heart and soul for more balance and happiness. My heavy workload and self-sacrifice had taken its toll once again and I began my pattern of questioning, but this time it was about my true heart's fulfillment, beyond money or professional success. For the very first time, I was interested in what made ***me*** happy. No doubt, my daughters and family are my priority; they are my heart and soul, but what was beyond that? My love of water! Being near water brings me unparalleled joy; it has always been my sanctuary for peace, tranquility, and introspection. Often as a little girl, I would retreat to a small creek near my home, sit on the sandy bank, and spend literally hours just listening to the soft trickle and just BE with nature! This childhood memory reminded me of my two previous visits to Kelowna, B.C. where I had felt at peace and secretly dreamed of retiring there one day. *Perhaps I should consider moving there?* I thought. *But it's too soon; I'm not ready to retire!* Then I asked myself: "Who says I can't do it now? Who's holding me back? What am I waiting for?"

So, once again, in 2014, I found myself taking another leap of faith and moving to the beautiful Okanagan! This time, my focus and intention were only on what brought me joy, rest and relaxation! This was my new priority and Kelowna, B.C. was my destination!

My journey in Kelowna had been an invaluable three-year healing experience before returning back to Calgary with a renewed sense of joy and purpose. The time spent by the water every day, the rest and relaxation, and the daily focus on happiness was exactly what my soul longed for to replenish and heal my body, mind and spirit. What made this journey so incredibly powerful was that it was the ultimate gift to myself. I had never done this before. Taking time for stillness allowed me to reflect on my life; to breathe, to just BE, to ask myself more meaningful questions, and to meditate on my needs, wants, and my journey. It allowed me to listen intently to my inner voice and guidance. As a result, I found clarity about what wasn't working and what could be improved so that I could finally design the life of my dreams. It was in the Okanagan Valley that I found the missing pieces for creating the life I desired! All these years, I had prepared for this; gathered the knowledge and the tools, put in the hard work, recognized my triggers, released old programming, healed my wounds, reflected more, dug deeper, listened to my inner messages, and recognized the synchronicities, but there was still more work to do! I had not yet released myself of remaining debt and I still longed to meet my soulmate. What were my next steps for creating the peace, joy, and freedom I dreamed of? After a long search, the answer became clear! It was PRACTICE!! What good was my knowledge if I didn't put it into practice? I had previously experienced results using my tools and processes, but I had not been consistent. All I needed to do now was to take action and did so until I succeeded!

It took just another six years for me to finally actualize the dream life I had always envisioned; one of inner peace, love and liberation. I feel so blessed and grateful for having unlocked the secrets to creating this life of joy and freedom. It is my mission today to awaken, empower, and support YOU in your journey to self-healing and self-love using these same invaluable tools and applications.

Today, I can honestly say I have ALL I ever wanted! Is there room for more? Absolutely! The possibilities are infinite, but every day, I have peace and gratitude in my heart, love and happiness all around me, and my "Grandeur Soul" guiding me. There is an ease and flow of life I trust, powerful tools for change, and a purpose and passion for helping others BE the change. But the most amazing love story of all is the "return to me;" my elevated self-love. I have come a very long way and count my blessings every day for having the awareness that being me ***is*** what I was always meant to be, and that infinite possibilities exist in life. Our choices and actions create change. You, too, effect change, my friend, simply by ***being*** YOU! The question is, who are you choosing to be? Are your choices creating happiness and the life you truly desire?

Infinite possibilities for your life await your command. YOU have the power to shape your reality in any way you choose! It starts with ***you*** and your ***conscious choice***. There is a Sioux saying: "The longest journey you will ever make in your life is from your head to your heart." I have come to understand that aligning these two is the key to self-love. The life of peace, happiness and freedom you seek are ***within*** you; it's an inside job! If you are ready, allow me to be your guide on your path. Never give up! Keep practicing your "return to me" muscle. Your ***best*** life is here for you now! Will you choose it?

Lessons Learned:

1. You have CHOICES! ***You*** are ethe only one who can CHOOSE the life you desire; no one else will do it for you. Embrace your greatness and BE the change you wish to see!
2. Do Not Doubt Yourself. *Listen* and *trust* your inner guidance; it will always lead you where you are meant to be.
3. Keep working your "Return to Me" (self-love) muscle!!! Peace, joy and freedom are when your heart, mind and soul are aligned and vibrating to the frequency of LOVE.

Mindset Tips:

1. Practice daily GRATITUDE. Begin your ***change*** process by writing three things you are grateful for every day, either before bed or first thing in the morning; this is when your subconscious is most receptive.
2. Take 10-20 minutes daily to VISUALIZE your ideal life, always keeping the end in mind. The Universe will always conspire to make it happen; listen to the whispers and take action!
3. Every day ***step away*** from your "busy" environment and just B-R-E-A-T-H-E. ***Visualize*** love and healing as you INHALE deeply… *hold for 5 seconds…* then ***visualize*** stress and tension leaving your body as you exhale fully. Repeat three times.

Aha Moments and Self-Reflections

Note your Thoughts

Jennifer Traynor

Jennifer Traynor is a writer and editor in Calgary, Alberta, where she lives with her husband, two children, and their family dog. While struggling with her mental health, she went on a journey of healing, self-discovery, and self-love. This prompted her to step forward to motivate and inspire other women to do the same. After nearly 20 years of working in corporate jobs, she took a leap of faith to start her own business and support other female entrepreneurs. She now works as a Strategic Storyteller by coaching businesswomen on how to get clear on their message and incorporate it into their content through strategic planning. Her goal is to help women use the power of storytelling to elevate their businesses and empower them on their road to success. In her spare time, Jennifer loves to practice yoga, read, do word puzzles, watch movies, and spend time with her family.

Connect with Jennifer:

https://linktr.ee/jennifertraynor

Chapter 8

How Losing My Job Was a Blessing

By Jennifer Traynor

They say the key to true happiness comes from within, and I know this to be true because I've learned it first-hand. Embarking on a journey to self-love helped me realize that I held the key to my happiness all along. But the reason I didn't see this before was that I was on a path of finding my joy from outside sources. I relied on attaining a well-paying job, an aesthetically nice home, and the validation of others to lead a happy life. Yet to no avail, I found myself miserable every day, never feeling fully satisfied with myself or my life despite the many blessings that I had. Want to know the pivotal moment that completely shifted my thinking and ultimately led to me realizing that I had gone about living a joyful life all wrong? Well, it was when I lost my job in 2018.

Ok, so you might be wondering how the negative experience of being laid off from a job that I loved could result in me shifting my mindset and beginning to live a happier life. And I totally understand why you would, since most people who are laid off don't look at it as a blessing. But for me, even though I didn't see it right away, losing my job was one of the best things that have ever happened to me.

To better explain this, I need to give you some background to this story. In 2017, after more than 15 years since graduating from college, embarking on a career to become a writer, and experiencing many failed attempts to do so, I was finally hired as a copywriter for an online parenting magazine. It was my dream job. I was working with a great team of fellow moms, collaborating on creating content, writing, and editing, plus working from home most of the time. This was what I had been waiting for. Needless to say, I was shaken to my core when less than a year later, I was unexpectedly laid off, along with most of the rest of my team.

I can still clearly picture myself sitting in my living room and bursting into tears after receiving the news over the phone. I sat alone in a daze for what felt like hours. Although my former boss assured me that this layoff had nothing to do with my performance as a writer, and had everything to do with the financial stability of the company, I felt like a complete failure. I felt so lost and didn't know what to do next.

I had been battling depression for a few years and had been doing better the past several months before the layoff. This turn of events prompted me to come undone. For the first few weeks, I had absolutely no motivation to do anything. I sat day after day, binge-watching shows on Netflix because I wanted to escape reality. I didn't want to face the fact that I was unemployed; I didn't want to endure the soul-sucking task of job hunting. I had done it many times before and it was mentally and emotionally exhausting. I was in no position to face rejection. But I knew that I couldn't avoid it forever, so after just over a month, I began searching for a job.

Days turned into weeks, which then turned into months. I sent out more job applications than I could count and was having no luck. With each passing day of not getting any calls or interviews, I became more and more defeated and my depression was getting worse. I found myself crying a lot and constantly beating myself up. *Stupid. Loser. Worthless. Not good enough.* This was all part of my internal dialogue and had been for many years. I had a lot of practice at being my personal punching bag because I had lived with low self-esteem for most of my life.

I can't quite pinpoint how and when it all started. I used to think that it stemmed from when I was picked on and tormented in grade school, and perhaps that's how it began. Though I can honestly say that when I reflect on my life from as far back as I can remember, there isn't one particular moment that stands out as to when my self-deprecation began. It just seems that somewhere along my journey, I completely lost a sense of who I truly was and convinced myself that I was a hopeless human being. I believed that I wasn't smart, talented, or beautiful, and had nothing worth offering this world. I was simply going through the motions of life, always feeling like an outsider looking in, and accepting that mediocrity was all I was going to achieve.

For much of my life, I didn't even like myself. I picked on everything about who I was. I didn't think I was pretty and never believed anyone would find me attractive. I struggled academically and felt stupid. I was clumsy and uncoordinated, so I didn't excel at anything remotely athletic. I was awkward and shy, so I had a challenging time making friends, and when I did, I still felt like I didn't belong. Being bullied as a child made me develop this need to feel hidden or just blend in. If nobody noticed the real me, then maybe they wouldn't notice what a loser I was.

Going through life believing that I wasn't good enough made it even easier for me to have a hateful dialogue running through my head when I was battling depression.

You're pathetic. You can't even get out of bed.

Some wife you are. You're always snapping at your husband.

You're a horrible mother. Stop shouting at your kids.

You're hopeless. Can you do anything right?

It was as though this dialogue ran on a loop, repeating itself over and over again. Nothing I did could shut it off. These thoughts weighed heavily on me and left me constantly feeling mentally and emotionally tired.

I actually wondered why my husband loved me and what he saw in me, and believed my children deserved a better mother. I remember admitting this to my husband once and telling him they would be better off if I wasn't in their lives. While he kept assuring me that it wasn't true, that he and the kids loved me and needed me, I had a hard time believing it. There were countless times when I thought of running away because I believed that I should spare them a life of living with a wife and mother who was angry, irritable, and sad all the time. But I didn't leave. Something within me was always telling me to just keep pushing forward. The truth of the matter was that I needed them more than they'll ever know. Despite thinking that my family would be better off without me, they were what kept me going; they were my motivation, whether they realized it or not. Without the love and support of my husband and children, I don't think I would be the woman I am today.

After losing my job, I ended up being unemployed for a year, and during that time, I did a lot of soul-searching. I was so tired of the constant darkness hovering over me. I needed to change, so I went to therapy, and I deepened my yoga practice by signing up for the 200-hour teacher training certification. At the beginning of 2019, nearly a full year after being laid off and countless hours of job hunting, I was offered a contract job. Although I wasn't entirely sure I was going to love it, I accepted the position. Even though I was considering the possibility of starting my own business, I figured that I could make some money working full-time while I sorted out what my next steps were and continued to do some work on myself.

Around the same time as starting this contract job, I began working with a life and business coach. This was when I started to peel back the layers and uncover some deeply-rooted truths about myself. For years, I had believed that it was likely being picked on by bullies as a child that created my low self-esteem; but the truth was that only one bully was doing the damage and that person was me.

The work I did with my coach and the other women in my coaching group, as well as the self-development, meditation, and self-reflecting that I did on my own, was what helped me realize what I had been doing to myself for so many years. These women helped me see that my inner dialogue was all lies and that it was time for me to discover my truth. It wasn't easy at first. I had a difficult time accepting compliments, let alone paying them to myself. But I made the commitment to myself that I was going to change. It was time for me to live a happier life, to recognize and acknowledge all the good things I had around me, and to be the woman that not only I deserved to be, but also the wife and mother my husband and children deserved.

Like so many other things we learn in life, learning to love myself took practice. I started with being more mindful; I wanted to become more aware of my thoughts and emotions, how I handled different situations and people, and how I viewed my surroundings. I made a point of trying to recognize the positive aspects of my day and being grateful for them, even if it was as simple as appreciating the sun shining. I got into the habit of pausing and taking cleansing breaths whenever I felt stressed because I had developed the bad habit of letting negative emotions get to me easily and reacting too quickly, often with regret. These little steps were a good starting point and made a great impact.

Next, I worked more on self-care. For a long time, I dealt with guilt whenever I wanted to sit back and relax, go to a yoga class, or go out with friends. I either felt bad for leaving the kids or kept stressing about the many things around the house that needed to be done. I continuously put the needs of others ahead of my own well-being and it left me feeling drained. Not only that, but I also found that I didn't really know who I was anymore. I had lost sight of my wants and interests. When it came to my never-ending to-do list, I always put myself last. It was time to make myself a priority. There's a reason why they say you can't pour from an empty cup. How could I put energy towards my self-care if I was always giving it away?

In time, it got easier to take breaks and focus on doing something I enjoyed. My husband and I made a pact that we would each take a night off every week to get out of the house for a few hours and do something just for ourselves. I started regularly going to yoga classes; meeting friends for drinks, dinner, or a movie; or sometimes just going to a coffee shop to sip a latte quietly while I read a book or did some writing. The more I did these things for myself, the more my cup was filled. I found myself looking forward to this weekly ritual and felt the guilt slip away with each passing week. I also noticed that I was finding more little things each day to be grateful for. Practicing self-care was giving me a new perspective on the world around me.

This self-care ritual also prompted me to look deeper within myself and closely examine who I was and what I truly desired. The more I reflected and meditated on this, the more I realized that, quite simply, what I really wanted in my life was happiness. I wanted to wake up every day and be happy with who I was; I wanted my family to be healthy and happy; I wanted a career doing something that I loved; and I wanted to help others be happy, too. I came across a simple Instagram post one day that said, "Today, I choose joy," and I decided right then and there that it would become my daily mantra.

I spent some time thinking about what this new mantra meant to me; what was choosing joy every day going to look like? I came to the conclusion that I would make an effort to always find something joyful in my day-to-day life, even on days when I might feel stressed, frustrated, sad, or angry. I didn't want to continue on the path of always defaulting to negative self-talk. Changing my dialogue was important to my journey to self-love, so even on my tough days if I could find one good thing to be grateful for, I knew it would positively impact my quest to live daily with joy.

As time went by, I noticed that I was slowly starting to appreciate different qualities about myself, and self-criticism was happening less frequently. It started with me recognizing my tenacity; no matter what life threw my way, I always seemed to pick myself up, dust myself off, and keep going. At one point, I felt like I was constantly facing struggles in my life and wondered if I was a glutton for punishment. I now viewed my determination to persevere as a strength.

The next change I noticed was how my mind shifted from always feeling sorry for myself—I can't tell you how many times the words "Why me?" went through my mind in the past—to now asking myself, "What can I learn from this?" or "What can I do differently?" whenever something didn't go exactly as I'd hoped. This was an important shift for me because I had spent many years of my life wondering why things never seemed to go my way.

One of the reasons that this change in mindset was such a big deal for me was because feeling sorry for myself played a large role in my struggle with depression. I was stuck in a "woe is me" state of mind for such a long time that it was difficult to break free from it. I found it challenging to see the bright side of life. I used to constantly compare myself to others and wondered why their lives seemed so much better than mine. When things didn't turn out the way I wanted them to, it was so easy for me to blame myself and come to the conclusion that I just wasn't deserving of something better.

By changing my mindset to viewing my life experiences as ways that I could learn and grow, I began to notice the fog of my depression slowly lifting, and I started realizing that my life wasn't as bleak as it seemed. Every day became a new learning experience for me and a new opportunity to let the real me shine through. It finally occurred to me that switching to a more positive way of thinking was going to help me break free from the wall of negativity I had put up around me. One way or another, that wall was coming down, even if I had to do it one brick at a time.

All of this inner work—practicing mindfulness, gratitude, and self-care; doing meditations and self-reflections; and shifting my mindset—has been crucial in discovering the real me and learning to love who I am. Getting to know myself has been an interesting journey. I have learned that I can be a critical thinker and that I am full of ideas. I'm good at problem-solving. I am intuitive and know that I can trust my gut instincts. I'm not as introverted as I once thought and quite enjoy socializing and meeting new people. I am fascinated by other people's stories and genuinely love to see others living happy lives. More importantly, I now know that I deserve a life of joy as well.

Discovering all of this about myself has given me the courage to pursue my dreams and do something that I'm passionate about. I have gained the knowledge and skills to do work that is meaningful to me and recognize that in doing so, I can inspire others. The woman who once saw herself as useless and wanted to hide in the shadows now stands proudly and knows her worth.

I have taken chances on myself that I never thought I would. I have left my corporate career behind in the pursuit of entrepreneurship and creating a business that I'm proud of. It may not be thriving—yet—but it is a creation that was born from life-long ideas, an imagination of endless possibilities, a passion and determination for doing something that I love and am good at, and the drive to inspire other women to embark on a similar journey.

I have awakened the woman who was always there, in the core of my being, in my soul, and am so grateful that I have found her. She is intelligent and strong, fierce and sassy, and beautiful inside and out. I wish I had taken the time to get to know her back then, but am thankful to be connecting with her now. It is never too late to form a deep connection with our inner selves.

When I reflect now on that day in 2018 when I was laid off from my copywriting job, I can see what an amazing gift that was. Had it not been for that experience, I may not have set out on a journey of self-development, self-reflection, mindfulness, gratitude, and self-love, and I quite possibly may not have learned these valuable life lessons.

This journey has taught me to be compassionate with myself, especially in my struggle with depression. Healing is an ongoing process and one that takes patience. I give myself grace when I have bad days and recognize when I need to take care of my mental health. I have learned that it's okay to not be okay and no longer view asking for help as a weakness. Self-care doesn't leave me guilt-ridden and is now an essential part of my being.

I have come to acknowledge that I am perfectly imperfect and embrace my flaws, yet I also know when to admit when I'm wrong and learn from my mistakes. I believe we should see value in our mistakes because they tend to hold some of the greatest lessons.

I am thankful for becoming more mindful, learning how to connect better to my feelings, and expressing my emotions. Developing a clearer awareness of the world around me has helped me see things from a different perspective. I find it easier to appreciate the little things in life and have discovered that it's the simpler moments that bring me the most joy.

When I think back to the person I once was—the little girl who felt stupid, the teenager who felt like an ugly outsider, and the young adult who felt worthless—my heart aches for the sadness that she felt, the days when she wished she could just disappear, and the anguish she endured. I wish I could go back and tell her that she was so much more than what her cruel inner voice kept telling her and that she was strong enough to push the darkness aside and let her light shine bright. Instead, I'm moving forward with pride in how far I've come and all that I've accomplished. And I like to think the old me would be proud, too.

So, you see, losing my job was a blessing; it completely changed the trajectory of my journey and sent me on a new path. Some may look at it as a new chapter in my story, but I see it as the start of my story and I've been writing new chapters ever since. There have been chapters about self-discovery, mindfulness, growth and learning, making mistakes and trying again, self-reflection, gratitude, self-care, acceptance, letting go, self-love, transformations, and possibilities. You might ask, "What's the next chapter?" I would tell you, but I can't yet because I'm still writing it. Although, I will tell you this: I love the woman I am today and who I am becoming, and I'm so excited to see where my story leads me next.

Three lessons that I have learned are:

1. Self-love starts with your inner voice. Once you change your inner dialogue to one that is kind and compassionate, loving yourself comes more easily.
2. Making mistakes in life does not make you less of a person. What you learn from your mistakes makes you stronger.
3. The true key to happiness in life comes from within. Self-love opens up a world of possibilities and joy.

Three mindset tips to share with others are:

1. To be successful is not to be without failure; it is to persevere through it.
2. Happiness does not come by chance; it comes by choice.
3. Learn to love yourself and let the rest fall into place.

Aha Moments and Self-Reflections

Note your Thoughts

Jostine Bulan

Jostine Bulan is a self-proclaimed wanderer who delights in following her heart's leading. After feeling the pull to focus on doing her Soul Work and Mission in 2022, she took certification classes for Reiki of the Usui System of Natural Healing and discovered her calling to be an energy healer.

Before she found Reiki, Jostine was already working with individuals as a life coach to help them love themselves wholly and live their lives fully. She has also facilitated life skills training for at-risk youths and positivity training for employees in the Philippines

A natural-born energy alchemist, Jostine holds a safe and sacred space for healing, expansion, and transformation to help others in their journey back to wholeness with themselves and oneness with life. Her work is centered on inviting others to be their fully expressed selves and co-creators of a more conscious world for us and the generations to come.

Connect with Jostine:

https://www.facebook.com/jostinebulan
https://www.youtube.com/@jostinebulan
https://linktr.ee/jostinebulan

Chapter 9

Free From Darkness at Last

By Jostine Bulan

During one of my Reiki self-healing practices, I was brought to a memory of writing the word "*tanga*" (stupid) on my left arm…

…not with a pen, but with a blade, cutting my skin and letting the words bleed out.

Up to this day, I still feel a twinge in my chest and a tightening in my gut whenever I go back to those days of cursing myself with so much hate.

"You are not enough."

"Why can't you die already? You're just a waste of space!"

"You're so stupid. Ugly. Unlovable. I hate you! It would be better for everyone if you were gone."

And the words that sealed my fate…

"I swear to God, no matter what, I will not live to reach my 20th birthday."

So, you can imagine the buckets of tears and intense crying that happened during that Reiki self-healing.

Amazingly, the movie in my mind shifted after releasing the pain and anger that had lived in my body for 30+ years. Instead of a blade, I was holding a permanent marker. Instead of cutting my skin, I drew Reiki symbols over the scars.

I felt God's infinite love and healing flowing through me and my past selves. That day, I finally felt truly free as I lovingly forgave myself for all the pain, curse, and hate towards myself.

I wish I could tell you it's that easy, but healing, forgiving, and loving myself have been full of twists and turns, bumps and dips, highs and lows. Starting with the most challenging step of all…

Facing My Inner Darkness

Light and darkness, I thank both.
For I wouldn't be here today
—doing the work that I'm doing—
had I not alchemized my darkness
and reclaim my Light within.
I wear the wisdom from lived experiences.
Of sitting intimately with my darkness
to embrace aspects of myself I disowned
and reclaim those I didn't even know.
It's been more than a decade-long journey
of unbecoming who the world said I should be
and ***being*** who my Creator envisioned me to be.
The journey continues.
(Oh, it will never stop!)
A one-of-a-kind journey that transcends lifetimes.

Self-love is a journey towards reclaiming our whole selves. It is loving the good, the bad, the beautiful, the ugly, and everything in between. It is knowing who we truly are and accepting all parts of ourselves. It's giving ourselves compassion and honoring our needs. Self-love is loving ourselves as we are—especially when we are in darkness.

I don't know when I started to be in love with myself, but my journey began in 2005 when I chose to live my life and gave myself a fighting chance. Before that, all I did was merely exist. Days were spent questioning why I was given this life and escaping to my imagined world. Nights were filled with silent tears pouring as I prayed for death to come. Everything felt meaningless. I was in a dark place, and I let that darkness consume me.

I was 13 years old when I started to cut myself. Before that, I was already cursing myself with hateful words that left deeper scars and fragmented parts of my being. My journey towards self-love has been filled with sitting in my darkness and meeting all aspects of myself, especially those I disowned in my childhood. It takes a tremendous amount of vulnerability to face my inner darkness. Allowing myself to be stripped down to my naked bones, letting go of identities that protected me as they kept me shackled.

These aspects of myself didn't reveal themselves all at once. One by one, they came to my awareness through people I met, triggers that disrupted my peace, memories that came out of the blue, and during my Reiki and meditation practice. Only when I met them in my darkness did I see these aspects of myself in a different light. I got to know them intimately. I saw how they have positively and negatively impacted my life. Seeing how they helped shape me into the person I am today opened my heart. I started falling in love with myself and reclaiming my beautiful, unique light.

But what does it even mean to face one's inner darkness?

For me, this means allowing myself to break down and cry. I trusted that going through my breakdowns was part of the rebirthing process. I went through several periods of disconnecting from the world so that I could hide in my cocoon and let myself go through the painful, yet necessary, transformational breakthrough. I uncovered and recovered parts of myself I didn't even know, discovering who I really am at my core. It was a process of unbecoming who the world said I should be and deconditioning myself from all expectations.

Facing my inner darkness has allowed me to see the limiting thoughts, stories, and patterns that ran rampant in my mind. Shining a light on my darkest moments has allowed me to release what doesn't belong and reclaim the fragmented parts of my soul. The more I go through this process, the more I experience love. Slowly but steadily, I started owning my power, gifts, and unique blend of magic.

Loving ourselves happens both inside and outside. I find it's easier to love ourselves when no other people are involved. It's easier to believe the new stories we claim for ourselves. We falter, however, when we go out in the world and get exposed to society's conditioning. This is okay and normal.

It took me years before I was able to love myself as I am, regardless of what's happening around me. I wouldn't be able to do it without surrendering to God and letting Him heal and embrace me with His love.

Receiving God's Infinite Love and Healing

Oh, how God's love and healing work in our lives.
Beautifully, wonderfully made—I AM.
I am God's masterpiece.
Chip by chip, He removes
pieces no longer serving me
To reveal the "Me"
He envisioned me to BE.
Purification. Healing. Releasing.
Removing anything, everything not aligned.
Bringing out the beauty that's already inside.
Linear, it is not.
Painful, it is much.
But God is lovingly, all-knowingly,
oh-so-carefully guiding the process along.
Shining Beautiful Soul,
If you could only see
the depth of awe and wonder
And love in your core…
I wonder how different
our lives could be
Standing
in our
Power
Truth
Sovereignty.

When I returned from the USA in 2015, I didn't know what to do next career-wise. I just knew I was called to help others, and I love personal growth and transformation. So, I looked for job openings, programs, and events related to personal growth. In my search, I somehow found Reiki. I immediately felt the pull to learn more, but as much as I wanted to attend classes, something always got in the way. Either I was unavailable during the scheduled classes, or I didn't have the budget to invest anymore.

"It's okay," I told myself. "All in God's perfect time."

Fast forward to 2021: Finally, the stars aligned! I was scrolling Facebook one Saturday morning when I saw an invitation for a free Reiki online healing. I was hesitant to attend at first because the event had already started, but something within was nudging me to go ahead and try it out. I learned to follow these nudges long ago because they never led me astray. In fact, following these nudges opened opportunities and life-changing experiences.

This time around was no different. After receiving Reiki for the first time, I felt my energy shifting and my heart opening up. I received healing and insight that day, which led to finding the right teacher and community for me to start my Reiki journey in 2022. Looking back, those seven years of waiting were necessary for this journey.

- During my time of waiting, I went through the following:
- Questioning whether I'm really called to have my coaching practice.
- Being financially broke and not knowing where to get the money to pay my bills.
- Trying my luck in juggling a full-time job and a coaching practice (and failing at it).
- Retreating and disconnecting from the world during the height of COVID-19 lockdowns, and feeling guilty that I wasn't doing my part in serving others.
- Learning to ask for help and be vulnerable with my financial situation.
- Trusting the pull to pause my coaching practice and get a full-time job again. This allowed me to get what I most need to strengthen my devotion to my chosen path.

I had to wait seven years, but in my years of waiting, I felt God's guidance and protection every step of the way. Even if I didn't understand why things were happening, I held on to the vision God put in my heart. It was truly a season of learning how to trust and surrender. And through Reiki, I was able to channel God's infinite love and healing to myself and others.

What I've come to realize is that healing comes in different ways. Sometimes, it's intense and dark. Other times, it's expansive and light. It also happens both on an individual and collective level. People and events that trigger us will reveal what is not in our awareness. There will be days when we will fall back to old patterns and limiting stories—these are all part of the healing process.

As we open our hearts to receive God's infinite love and healing, we learn to love all aspects of ourselves and who we truly are at our core—wholly, fully, and unconditionally. Genuinely loving ourselves naturally evolves into loving all of life and humanity as separateness from others dissolves.

We see beyond our little world and expand our perspective to know that we are part of a bigger whole. In loving ourselves, we also raise the collective frequency of love on the planet. We become co-creators of a brighter world for us and the generations to come.

Expanding My Possibilities

This week, my self-healing continues.
Trusting myself more.
Trusting God to fully support me.
With that, shadow aspects of myself arise.
Fragmented parts of my Soul,
ready to come home and be integrated.
Bringing love to my Inner Child

as I reparent her and be the parent
I needed when I was young.
Healing my relationship with receiving
money, success, accomplishments, and fame.
Allowing Life to fully support me.

In the Philippines, it's common to follow a path set forth by one's family, especially if you are the oldest child. There's an expectation (whether vocally expressed or not) for children to go to school, get good grades, graduate, get a job, get married, have their own family, and take care of their aging parents.

One of the children will take in their parents to care for them. If you're the oldest child, there's an added expectation to take on the breadwinner's role in the family as soon as you finish school and get a job. Those in less privileged families usually don't go to college (or school at all), so they can work and help support the rest of the family.

Filipinos greatly value family. Sometimes, even to the point of sacrificing our own needs to keep peace and harmony. I wrestled with this growing up. Ever since I can remember, I questioned why I was given this life. I wished that I could follow the path of being a good daughter and fulfilling my role in the family. But there was only emptiness in me. I felt like a burden and a waste of space because I couldn't see a future for myself.

During my darkest moments, I remember praying to God to give my life to someone who needs it more; someone who is making a difference in this world, and is more deserving and worthy. I thought it was a noble prayer, yet it remained unanswered. So, I took matters into my own hands.

One Saturday morning, while I was alone in my dorm room, I was ready to end it all. The pain of believing I was just a waste of space and couldn't amount to anything had become unbearable. I didn't have it in me to fight another day. I was ready. I was holding my blade in my right hand. My hands were shaking as I cut deeper, deeper, and deeper. In the middle of my quiet gut-wrenching sobs, I heard a small still voice telling me:

"Just hold on for one more day. Hold on."

I didn't know why or where I got the strength that day, but I heeded that voice. I held on even though I didn't know what tomorrow would bring. I held on. I didn't know it then, but that day, I did kill my old self by choosing to hold on—saying yes to my new becoming. It was the beginning of reclaiming who I came here to be as I paved my own path and lived my life anew.

I wish it was fairy tales and rainbows after that rebirth. I knew deep in my soul that I was following the path that lights me up and makes me come alive. However, I carried the guilt and shame of following my own path. In my "selfishness," I couldn't contribute financially to my family yet. The thing that pains me the most? There was a genuine desire for me to give my mom a comfortable life. I want to be able to treat my mom and sister to experiences that we've only dreamed of, like traveling and dining, without thinking about the price.

It's so easy to fall into the trap that I was self-serving in loving and choosing myself first. But I've come to realize that I can do the deep work with my clients because I have gone through the trenches of my darkness and put my own needs above all. I can hold the space for others' healing, expansion, and transformation because I was able to hold this space for myself first. I can serve others without depleting myself because I am filling my cup and serving from my overflow.

I felt so lost in my younger years; however, I was lost in the right direction because my soul had been navigating the way all along! Learning this truth, plus my daily practice of self-healing, allowed me to release feelings of guilt and shame for following my path and doing what feels good and right for my well-being. I'm also trusting that as I continue to follow the path of my highest contribution, God is in charge of taking care of me and my family.

It's been almost two decades of focusing on my personal growth and transformation, choosing myself first and paving my own path, and holding space for my own healing, expansion, and transformation. I am now ready to play full out and say yes to the mission of helping others be who they came here to be so they can step into their fullest and highest expression in this lifetime.

Expressing My Truth

I release any and all expectations
of who I should be, what I should be,
and how things should be.
Owning my Truth.
Taking my rightful place.
Standing in my Power.
Embodied wisdom.
Fully expressed.
I AM.

I remember talking with my friend, Andrea, about how we are called to serve life. When it was my turn to share, I felt a tightening in my chest and heaviness in my shoulders. Deep down in my soul, I knew I was called to help transform people's lives. I knew that even though I'd rather support others in the background, I was called to step out of the shadows to share my message on a bigger platform.

I cried that day because I felt the call, but it also felt so heavy. My friend lovingly told me it was okay to be in this space, and it was okay if I was not yet ready to answer that bigger call. We all have our own timing and pacing, and God knows this. Doing our life's work is not meant to be heavy and constricting. Instead, it is intended to be expansive and freeing.

That conversation happened in 2021. Now, I am happy to share that whenever I think of the mission God has entrusted me, I feel the excitement coursing through my veins. I feel so alive and lit up. I am finally ready to go all in.

So, what changed?

It's years of doing the inner and outer work, plus God's grace and healing, as well as allowing myself to show up as I am, especially when feeling down and low.

It's years of choosing to grow through my discomfort and giving myself permission to fail, make mistakes, and be misunderstood by others as I intentionally step into my courage and do things that scare the shit out of me.

It's years of letting myself be with my darkness, owning my light, putting myself out there, and choosing to follow the pull of inspiration even though I didn't know what would come out of it.

It's the culmination of all those steps that built my unshakeable faith and trust in God—leading me to live a life of surrender and allowing.

With God's grace and guidance, Reiki continues to help me heal, release, and transmute the energies of what's no longer serving me. It feels like I am receiving an accelerated spiritual upgrade! The battle between my old self and the person I'm becoming has suddenly stopped. There is only loving acceptance of all that I am. I didn't have to choose between the two because I learned to hold space for both. When I stopped battling with myself, that's when I felt truly free to be me at my fullest and highest expression.

It's like a switch turned on, and I am releasing the expectations from myself and others. I am free to be me because I am enough as I am. I can own my unique gifts, take space, embody my power, and speak my truth. This is such a huge thing coming from an INFP and Enneagram 9w1, who would rather observe in the background and let others take the stage. But I also know we are here to transcend labels and weave our own stories.

So, I am choosing to be seen, heard, and experienced by others, and to share my gifts in service of the highest good. Through my courageous sharing, I hope to inspire others to be fully expressed as well. That said, this is still a growth area for me. I already feel aligned energetically. It's now time to put this into practice. And so, the journey continues…

Final Words

The new me is stepping into her leader and teacher energy:

She is taking her space and asserting herself—owning her energy, voice, and presence.

She speaks with clarity, conviction, and confidence—owning her gifts, superpowers, and sovereignty.

She is unapologetic in paving her own way and shining her light—trusting herself and the wisdom from her lived experiences.

She opens herself as a channel and messenger for God's joy, peace, love, light, healing, and abundance—knowing she can never mess this up because this is her birthright.

With God's guidance, protection, and providence, she continues her journey to be all she can be and do what she came here to do.

This is what I'm choosing to devote my life to. By loving myself wholly and living my life fully, I can show up as the conscious co-creator that I am and unleash my unique magic!

Lessons Learned:

1. This life is a journey of unbecoming who the world said we should be and becoming the person our Creator envisioned us to be.
2. I am Divinely guided, protected, and provided for. Always.
3. In holding space for both my light and darkness, I am able to heal, release, and transmute what is no longer serving me.

Mindset Tips:

1. What if there is no one right path, and you can never get it wrong because your soul is navigating the way all along? Play with this question and see what will open up for you.
2. Loving ourselves is a choice and a commitment that we make every single day to choose what will serve our highest good. Write a vow to yourself and describe in as much detail as possible what loving yourself looks like for you.
3. Going through periods of darkness is part of the rebirthing process. It may feel like you've been buried, but it's a stage of going into your cocoon and evolving into your next level of expansion. What support do you need to help navigate this transition?

Aha Moments and Self-Reflections

Note your Thoughts

Kamilla Harra

Kamilla Harra is a Light Guidance channel, and a soul-led joy and purpose coach and mentor who helps people embody their authentic selves, so they can become naturally confident, have happier relationships, and bring their best to the world.

She studied Psychology at Trinity College Dublin, Ireland, and is also a preferred PSYCH-K® facilitator, Systematic Kinesiologist, and Sacred Sound & Light healer. Kamilla studied Nutrition, EFT, and multiple holistic modalities to help people heal and step into their full power. She is the originator of Conscious Wholeness™ healing modality.

Kamilla appeared on TV3's 'How Healthy Are You? and TV3 Saturday AM Show in Ireland, taught living nutrition internationally for seven years, wrote for the *Green Living NZ* magazine, *Organic NZ Magazine*, and appeared on *English Talks 2017: The Brain 1000 Inspiring Ideas*. In the last 16 years, Kamilla has helped over 2,000 people let go of being worried, doubtful, and uncertain to find a greater purpose, wellness, and joy in their lives.

Connect with Kamilla:

https://linktr.ee/kamillaharra
https://soulsradiance.org/

Chapter 10

Didn't Know I was Lost Until I Found Me

By Kamilla Harra

Each one of us comes into this world with a chance to fully embody self-love and lovingness in the most wonderful ways. Yet, we also experience a separation from love during times of pain and suffering; these are dark periods when we feel lost, forgotten, unimportant, and unwanted. On these pages, I'm sharing my journey from separation into the wholeness of love through some extraordinary events and surprising realizations.

For at least a decade of my life, I deeply disliked myself and much of the world around me, and it was strange that I had no idea I felt that way. My awakening from the dream of ignorance and self-dislike was sudden and very shocking, and so was my discovery that the support of love was always there for me and everybody else. I know that's why I am unshakable today.

I was eighteen and sitting in the study room of the Psychology Department at Trinity College Dublin in Ireland. It was my first year of doing a degree in Psychology. The hushed room was cozy as I sat reading through and filling out multiple questionnaires for Abnormal Psychology. In the chapter I was reviewing, it detailed ways of testing individuals for certain personality traits, as well as determining whether somebody was on a "disorder spectrum." I was reading the section that listed examples of questionnaires for clinical depression. As I started answering questions, I noticed something unusual: my answers decidedly leaned toward the "depressed" end of the scale.

With each further question, without exception, I saw that my inclinations, feelings, motivations, and thoughts were not what I'd believed about myself until then—a balanced and rational 18-year-old. Instead, my answers pointed toward a diagnosis of depression. With a growing feeling of heaviness in my chest, I tried a different questionnaire just to be sure, but it gave me the same grim results: I took no pleasure in life activities, had little genuine interest in anything, was unenthusiastic about my future, mostly felt empty, often sad, and sometimes angry. I was generally cynical and seldom emotional; life seemed meaningless and I wasn't too excited about being alive.

As my eyes scanned these words on the page, it felt as though darkness engulfed me, narrowing down to just a sliver of light and all that remained was the book and me. I felt a wave of nausea twist in my stomach, my heart started to beat very fast, its rhythm loud in my head—bang, bang, bang, bang!

Taking deep breaths, I willed my mind to think and analyze what was happening. Some of what I read wasn't that new to me. I had been already aware that I was generally reserved and not very excited whether things went well or badly for me—I thought I was stoic! I was also very serious and didn't enjoy the usual things teenagers did, such as hanging out in large groups, drinking, or going to concerts; I thought I was just a bit more mature and introverted. What was complete news to me was that depression wasn't just about "crying all the time and feeling sad;" it turned out to be more about numbness, lifelessness, and joylessness.

Over the next twenty minutes, my mind rounded off quite a different newly revealed reality of what it was like to be me, complete with proof as multiple memories surfaced. I recalled an abrupt "shutting" of my previously widely open loving heart at the age of eleven (triggered by an abusive event), my long-standing general anxiousness, a total lack of real joy in life, and a particularly chilling memory of riding a bus home from school when I was thirteen, and feeling so hopeless and disinterested that I contemplated finishing off my life!

I was faced with a horrible, unavoidable truth about myself and it was scary because it felt like I no longer knew who I was, or, worst of all, if I was even "normal."

I got up, packed my books, and walked slowly out of the building. Everything seemed a blur around me, unreal and unfamiliar. I was walking in a strange and sickly bubble of misery and shock. Noises faintly happened out there in the world, outside my bubble, as people's shadows hurriedly passed by. Just before exiting the college grounds, I had to lean against the wall as a deeper wave of confusion and despair hit me. It was scary to move my identity from my usual good self to somebody weird, unrecognizable, and unwell.

However, by the time I started crossing the road leading away from the college, my mind had accepted my new reality: *So, I am depressed.* As this clicked into place, I felt calmer and my choices became clear.

It seemed I had two options: the first was to go to my class tutor, who was a psychotherapist offering free counseling to all Psych undergrads. As I contemplated it, I remembered my mom, a doctor who had multiple ill-health labels and was constantly "treated" for them. She put all her hopes and dreams into the hands of her colleagues to fight her labels for her. A huge wave of "NO!" swelled up and crashed within me; this option meant becoming a victim of a diagnostic label in the outer world, instead of changing how I felt inside. It meant placing how I felt entirely under somebody else's control and guidance—if they succeeded at "fixing" me, I would feel better; if not, I'd stay unwell. This was just not for me! This realization was so powerful, it almost made me physically jump in the middle of the road. The second option pointed at an awareness that something within ***me*** caused me to be this joyless. I was the one who needed to discover what I'd done and reverse it; as I already knew my way into depression, all I needed to do was to turn back and retrace my steps out of it. The resolve solidified and I swore to myself that I would find out how to change my feelings for the better. By the time I stepped onto the pavement on the other side of the street, I was steady, energized, and determined. *

**Disclaimer: I fully believe that everybody has their own way of healing and their own unique journey here—be it with psychotherapy, hypnosis, regression, coaching, and many other ways. In my life following that day, I worked with some amazing professionals when I felt it was right for me. However, regarding that particular part of my journey to self-discovery and love, I knew I needed to do it the way I did.*

Within twenty-four hours, I worked out what was missing for me. Everybody who was genuinely lively, enthusiastic, and joyful had one thing in common: each of them was uniquely interested in something in the world. Every person, without exception, who was truly "happy" knew what they liked and pursued it.

It seemed that they had these unique inclinations almost from birth, independent of their genes, gender, nurture, or culture. I even recalled my childhood friends from kindergarten; as young as three-years-old, they had individuated curiosity and enthrallment with life. As they grew up, they either accepted and followed where their essential nature led them, or they adopted other people's interests and were a bit like me—flat and uninspired.

As I pondered the best word to describe this uniqueness within each person, the one that came to mind—to my huge surprise—

was Soul! At eighteen, I laughed at religious terms, as I was arrogant enough to consider myself too educated to believe in such nonsense. However, at that moment "soul" felt like exactly the right term. I thought to myself: *I, too, must have my specific spark of life interest, but as I have no idea what it is, I must be disconnected from my soul! I need to reconnect with it as soon as possible so that I know what makes me feel alive!*

Over the two years that followed, I diligently paid attention to and got increasingly more curious about how I felt at all times, so I could find out what made me "tick" and made me happy. With practice, I began to experience my feelings most of the time, noticing what genuinely brought me joy! Gradually, the fog of indifference, disinterest in life, and a sense of dread lifted—I knew I was no longer depressed and that I would never be again in this life.

Little did I know that this was just a tiny step in the direction of rediscovering my true nature.

My next major step towards self-discovery was stunningly surprising and like nothing that I had ever experienced before. It happened in Spain when a group of us went to a wedding in Barcelona (where I also discovered my love for dancing, alcohol-free and non-stop until sunrise). We hired a car and took a trip to the Basque country. We drove across most of the north of Spain to the ancient coastal town of St. Sebastian. It was truly breathtaking there: tall cliffs wrapped in lush greenery framed the terracotta roofs of the seaside town, while narrow cobbled streets wound tightly around elegant sandstone buildings. We were trying to find the oldest church in town when I suddenly noticed it—as though it was stubbornly squeezed between two other buildings—a gorgeous baroque facade that was clearly a church. The St. Maria Basilica del Coro was tiny yet very ornate, and thinking this might be the place we were looking for, I ventured in.

Once inside, I immediately stepped onto somebody's feet! From the entrance and as far as the eye could see, there were so many people that I could barely wedge in and close the door behind me. The people were gazing upward toward the high elegant curves of the sandstone vaulted ceiling, and they were all... singing! The sound engulfed me and in the next moment, I had an experience like no other before; it felt as though I was lifted into a huge space of pristine and pure hope and love. My body felt weightless and disappeared into this timeless other-worldliness. I was rising and expanding in a blissful awareness of joy and freedom! There were no thoughts as I felt one with this pure, peaceful, majestic, and overwhelmingly pleasant field of light. After some time, my mind stirred into thinking and questioned what was happening—immediately a word blossomed upon the blank canvas of my consciousness as the Universe whispered the answer back: g r a c e...

I had never used the word "grace" before. I did not even fully understand what it was supposed to mean, as I grew up in a country without religion. But at that moment, I understood that it was otherworldly, harmonious, luminous, divine, uplifting, indescribably blissful, and beyond the heaviness that I habitually lived with.

That experience changed me forever.

I realized that this otherworldly, out-of-body, blissful experience was possible because many people came together intentionally to connect with and express divine love, purity, and grace. Two things amazed me: that something so incredible could actually exist and that people could "summon" it on purpose!

This recognition started to heal some very painful feelings and limiting beliefs I'd held about life from a very young age. From as little as three years old, I used to feel very sad and disappointed looking up at adults and I'd silently wonder: *Where is the kindness here? Why is it so low? Why aren't they being fully loving and warm like they could be?* The loving grace at the Basilica showed me a deeper reality behind what I experienced as a child; love was here and people could live in it fully and completely! The happiness and fulfillment that many were deeply yearning for was love itself, and we were all able to embody love when we focused our attention on it. We could then become the fullest expression of our nature: conscious, kind, loving, creative, life-affirming, joyful, and sacred beings of immense power. Everything less, all unkindness, came as a result of a separation from love.

I was now certain that I lived in a kind Universe, whose love was untapped and unused by humans in everyday life, and this could change if enough of us wanted to feel this wonderful feeling on purpose, together! I longed for all of us to rediscover and start choosing our innate lovingness to transcend the need for fear, pride, and anger. And so, I set out on a big learning quest.

I spent my twenties and thirties researching ancient and contemporary mystics and yogis, quantum physics, sacred geometry, extrasensory perception, multiple healing modalities, energy medicine, shamanic teachings, and practiced meditation, including Vipassana and the Sacred Heart activation. This still didn't feel enough, so I studied holistic, developmental, and social psychology, EFT, PSYCH-K™, nutrition, and kinesiology because I realized that when we felt better physically, mentally, and energetically, it was easier to accept and embody our true loving nature.

As I studied and practiced, new interesting abilities opened up within me as though my loving self was allowed to show up more and more in everyday life. At first, I was able to accurately sense other people's feelings and subconscious beliefs, which helped them heal at much deeper levels. Later, I began to intuitively receive detailed information about the best approach each person in front of me could take to feel better and lead a happier life. In my late twenties, a most wonderful ability spontaneously showed up. I became aware of knowing how to direct my voice to sing or speak melodiously to release heavy energies in people's bodies and minds and fill them with the frequencies of love and grace. (I later studied sound healing in order to logically understand how it worked). This was pure magic because I could feel that I was now doing something similar to the incredible lightness I experienced in the Basilica in St. Sebastian!

Since that time, I recognized that love has been guiding and supporting me all along, and that self-love has allowed this guidance to come to all parts of me, no matter how they felt. I have also become a joyful facilitator to people reconnecting with their own unique loving selves. As this happens, people feel more energized, inspired, loving, and courageous; they often say they come home to who they truly are! This excites, humbles, and moves me deeply! It is hard to imagine that at some point, I considered this existence and my life pointless. I have moved from being somebody unhappy, carrying a lot of pain, and feeling detached from love, people, and life, to a woman who now appreciates the human and spiritual parts in herself and others; she enjoys herself a lot more and lives with a bright spark of love in her heart.

Where I felt lost, there is now an unshakable unity with all beings on this planet and with the underlying intelligent kindness that runs through all and manifests as everything—Love.

Wisdom Nuggets:

1. **Self-curiosity is crucial for self-love, happiness, and fulfillment.** Paying attention to my emotions allows me to feel that I truly care for myself. This makes me feel seen, heard, accepted, and loved, and makes life interesting and enjoyable!

2. **Accepting our uniqueness is a gateway to loving ourselves unconditionally.** When we ignore our uniqueness, we feel unloved, unworthy, and lonely because we cannot get to know and love ourselves authentically. By welcoming our individuality, we can return from feeling **unwanted, desperate, and lost to feeling joyful, worthy, and capable of success.**

3. The Universe is governed by love and harmony. It would cease to function coherently if it was run by anything less than that. **Feeling unlovable or unloving is a part of the human experience. It gives us a chance to learn sovereignty and free will by choosing to love consciously, even when others may not.**

4. **Self-love is a conscious choice** and an ability to attune to the highest frequency of kindness, acceptance, and love with zero judgment. It is when all that I am is received, heard, seen, allowed, honored, and loved by all that I am with unconditional love and kindness.

How to Increase Love and Natural Happiness in Your Life:

1. Learn to notice and feel your emotions without judgment, so you can bring every part of yourself back into love: Most people cannot let go of past pain and self-dislike because they don't even know they hold them. Often there is a fear around feelings because of the sheer unfamiliarity with what it's like to feel the emotions and be okay with that. As a result, many overfocus on thoughts, so their emotions play out subconsciously, thus causing unhappiness and self-sabotage.

Exercise: At least once a day, sit down, close your eyes, and take a breath. Feel the weight in your body. Focus your mind on your feet, then the palms of your hands, and then your chest. Place your hands on your chest. Notice your heartbeat. Notice emotions rising in your chest: Are you peaceful? Are you a little restless? Maybe even anxious? Or annoyed, excited, loving, scared, apprehensive, afraid, worried, frustrated, angry, indifferent, numb? Simply observe with minimal thoughts and no judgment for 2-3 minutes.

2. Question your "shoulds" to act in alignment with love: If you work with people, then making others happy might be a part of your job, but if you keep "should-ing" yourself into actions 24/7, you are ignoring your essential loving self. "Should" can take you away from knowing what actions are really loving to you. It comes with a sense of guilt or obligation and is not about genuine love for you or other people. Whenever I used to say "I should or I shouldn't," I paused and rethought if it was actually true. The answer was always the same—it could only be true if I believed it was, so there was no universal "should."

Exercise: Once a week, contemplate or write down all activities that make you happy, whether other people know about them or not. Notice if there is any "should, must, or need to" in these activities. We were taught that meeting goals other people love doing or approve of will make us happy, but lasting joy comes from carrying out activities with no "should" in them—just your personal want, interest, joy, and fun!

3. Practice being caring and compassionate to yourself: Being loving towards all of your natural human states—such as fear, anger, sadness, and apathy—helps form a steady love you can lean into as a loving, warm, and kind environment within. All humans experience these feelings, so it doesn't mean you are bad, weak, or wrong.

Exercise *(based on Kristin Neff's work)*: Whenever you notice that you are struggling in any way, leave the self-judging attitude aside and imagine you are speaking to yourself as your greater self or soul—the loving, generous, and accepting one. **Say silently or out loud:** *"I love you, and it's okay that you're feeling this. All people feel these feelings; this is normal and I accept how you feel. I'm sorry you feel bad. I am holding you. It is going to be okay. This will pass and is not who you are. There is no rush; I am with you as you feel this. I love you."*

4. Reconnect with your natural state of being loving: Our spiritual nature is love, by consciously inviting love into our body, mind, and emotions and focusing on it, we start to not only feel better but heal the deep separation between our human and spiritual parts of self.

Exercise: Sit down comfortably. Take a deep breath, let it out through your mouth, and let go of your thoughts. Imagine your thoughts moving away from you like little birds. Now there is more space within your head and body for you to just be. Take a breath and imagine you are inhaling light into yourself. Hold that breath, and see the light spread through your chest, head, and limbs. Exhale and see the light reaching the outer edges of your body. Take another breath like that and see how the light gets brighter when you hold your breath and exhale. Now inhale the light and all the love in the world—hold your breath, and imagine the warmth of love and light nourish and soothe your heart; as you exhale, it's helping you let go of everything that isn't loving. Take another breath of loving light and bring your hands to your chest; feel your hands send love into your heart as you hold your breath. See the love becoming stronger and brighter in your chest and hands. As you exhale, feel the warmth of love spread through your body, healing and resolving all challenges and problems within you so there is only love between all parts of your mind and body. Inhale the love into your heart and see that it's activating your own loving nature deep within it; every cell, every molecule, and atom is dancing with love, and spreading this love through your chest and body. As you exhale and spread the loving light, think to yourself: ***I am open to more and more love. I love and I am loved.*** Take another breath of love, hold it, and repeat the same. Keep doing this until you feel nourished again by love.

*With the purchase of this book, you can ask for audio recordings of these exercises through my website: soulsradiance.org

Lessons Learned:

1. Self-exploration is essential for lasting happiness and fulfillment.
2. You need to follow your individual life interests or you lose your joy.
3. The Universe is unconditionally loving and you can experience this love at will.

Mindset Tips:

1. Get curious about and attentive to your emotions, this will let you know what you need, so you can take better care of yourself.
2. Use self-compassion to regulate challenging emotions when you feel out of sorts.
3. Practice meditations designed to increase love in your heart

Aha Moments and Self-Reflections

Note your Thoughts

Kara O'Daniel

Kara O'Daniel is from St. Louis, Missouri. She has two amazing parents, two wonderful siblings, and a huge extended family that is extremely supportive. She is the client concierge for Dr. Erin Oksol. Her fiancé, Jon, and his two sons make her world a better place to live in. She loves to read books, binge-watch Netflix and Hulu, spend time with her nieces and nephew, and play video games with her mother-in-law. She has always had a very strong faith and believes that this is what has helped her through her darkest times. She is the founder of *Seek the Heart*, a movement that helps others who have faced challenges in life due to health issues or disabilities to realize their value and self-worth and become their best self! And, to inspire these individuals to, in turn, use their stories to help others. She believes advocacy is so important! Kara is also the co-founder of the Academy of St. Louis.

Connect with Kara:

https://linktr.ee/karaodaniel

Chapter 11

If Psych Wards Had Punch Cards

By Kara O'Daniel

If psych wards had punch cards, my next visit would be free. To date, I have been in the psych ward eight times. Most people think of psych wards as torture; a kind of hell on earth. For me, they were where I was most safe. There is someone always watching your every move, there is nothing there you can harm yourself with, and everyone is there for themselves, so you don't feel judged (or there was always someone crazier than me so that made me feel "normal"). I was crippled with debilitating depression for nearly 20 years. Last month, before I turned this chapter in, my therapist, whom I have seen weekly for eight years, told me I could come on an as-needed basis because I am happy, joyous and free!

The dictionary defines self-love as regard for one's well-being and happiness. I love this definition because it encompasses the whole self. In order to truly love yourself, you must take ownership of your mind, body and spirit. You cannot be truly happy unless you love yourself. I'm excited to be sharing how I transformed into the person I am today and how I came to truly understand and feel self-love. It is my hope that after you are done reading this chapter, you have a new understanding of self-love, and if you struggle with it, that you can learn to love yourself, just as I did! I am living my best life and I cannot wait to share the ways my life transformed so that you, too, can love yourself and live the best life you can on this earth!

I remember like it was yesterday. I was in sixth grade and I fought with myself daily. I struggled to get out of bed, to have the energy to go to school, and to gain the strength to want to live. What kept me going was my friendship with a girl named Julie. I don't know if y'all remember back in the day when AOL instant messenger (AIM for short) was a thing. Every day after school, I would get on AIM and talk to Julie for hours. She was the one who kept me afloat. She didn't know it at the time, but her friendship meant everything to me. To this day, I don't think that I would still be around if it wasn't for her.

One night that same year, I was laying in bed —I had no self-esteem, self-confidence, or self-love. I quite literally hated myself—and I texted my twin brother, Kyle, and told him that I wanted to die. I think the text was something like this: "Don't tell anyone but I don't want to live anymore." Kyle was and will always be my best friend and biggest support. Of course, he told my parents right away. They immediately came back to my room; we had a discussion and came to an understanding that I was not in immediate danger. I was having horrible thoughts but I was 100% not going to act on them. The next morning, my mom reached out to a therapist to get me help.

Sending that text to my brother changed everything. I don't think words can describe the hurt I was feeling. I felt utterly hopeless and helpless; as though I were a huge burden on everyone around me, and I was completely empty inside. Imagine the worst sadness you have ever experienced and multiply that by five; that was how I felt. I was dead inside, but then I started working with a therapist and things started getting better.

I was 20-years-old the first time I visited a psych ward. I was desperate and didn't feel safe being out in the world, despite my family being so supportive and knowing they would have watched me every moment of every day to make sure I was safe. It still was not enough. I needed help, and I needed it right away. I felt safe the moment I stepped into the psych ward. It's a funny feeling because there are some absolutely insanely sick people in there, and some of them can get pretty aggressive. Even with those people there, I still felt it was a safe place. I knew I was there to get better and I just had to focus on that.

The three things that I think are vital to self-love are: finding your purpose on the planet, living in an environment that you can thrive in, which includes having an incredible support system of friends and family around you, and taking care of your mental health. Before going into the hospital, I didn't really feel like I had a purpose. I was just going through the motions of the day. Sure, I loved being a nanny and did so for many different families. It truly brought me joy, yet there was something missing. I wouldn't fully understand what that was until almost eight years later.

I was in and out of psych wards throughout my twenties. The first time I was ever in the psych ward was when my grandfather had passed away and at the same time, I had a miscarriage. My grandpa was one of my best friends. We always had so much fun together. Most people don't know about my miscarriage because I have kept it a secret. I also kept my pregnancy a secret from everyone, except for Kyle and his wife, Cassy. I felt ashamed because I was taught not to have sex until after marriage. I felt embarrassed and scared to death that my parents would hate me. I know, it's ridiculous. Anyone who knows my parents knows that they would never hate any of their children, no matter what they did.

I actually started having a miscarriage the day I went to tell my parents I was pregnant. It was all just too much. The psych ward was my only option, so I went and was in for two and a half weeks. While I was there, they gave us a self-assessment in one of the groups they were giving. It was basically to see how well we viewed our life at that moment. The purpose was to take inventory of how you were feeling so that you could begin to work on getting better. It was a 0-10 assessment. I scored everything from a 1-3. My mind was in a really dark spot. The doctors finally found a combination of medication that worked for me and I was sent home.

I would go in and out of the psych ward many more times. I was starting to feel like it was a never-ending cycle. However, there was hope! I met this guy in the psych ward during the seventh time I was there. You know, because dating a person you meet in the psych ward is a really good idea. Now, I can look back and think to myself, "What was I thinking?!" But back then my thought was, "Well, he is in here too, so he probably understands a little of what I am going through." He and I ended up dating for a year.

We actually had some really amazing times together, until we didn't. I am not going to sit here and tell you everything that went wrong in our relationship, because in the end it just doesn't matter. At the time of our break up, we had an apartment together and we had to figure out how things were going to work until our lease was up. God helped me out in a huge way with the two things that happened next.

It had been a couple of months and we still had our apartment together, but he was not living there full time. One night while I was out with my grandma, I got a call from my apartment complex. They had informed me that my apartment flooded. I rushed back to my apartment because my cat, George, was in there and I wanted to see what the damage was. Inches of water covered the entire apartment and everything was soaked. Thank God for renter's insurance! It took weeks to get it all cleaned up and straightened out with the insurance, but eventually, everything was taken care of.

During all of this, I was having a really hard time getting over my break up. One day, I was talking to his mom, (Side note: she and I got along until the day she sadly passed away) and she told me I needed to get on Tinder to get over her son. I was immediately taken aback and said "No way! Tinder is a hook-up app and I am ***not*** into that." Then, the next day it snowed. I was bored, so I bargained with myself to make a Tinder account. Afterall, Tinder is just a picture and a one-sentence bio about you, so it didn't take long to make. I gave myself one hour to see what kind of men I could attract. Six minutes in, my life changed forever. I met my fiancé, Jon, who has helped me encompass everything it means to truly love yourself in ways I never knew was possible. More on him a little later.

At this point, I had been in and out of the psych ward, working with a therapist weekly on my self-esteem and how to cope with life, and taking medication to keep me from having depressive episodes. Not only did I have a long track record of being in the psych hospital, I have had 49 surgeries to date. My first surgery was when I was just a couple hours old due to a birth defect called Spina Bifida. I have been a tough person since I was a little girl. I handled all the surgeries and recoveries like a champ and I very rarely complained. It was just part of who I was. The more surgeries I had, the more I realized that the surgeries were becoming part of my identity. This did not help with loving myself.

While I was having to go in and out of hospitals my whole childhood, I was also dealing with bullying at school. I believe that the bullying is why I had my first suicidal thought at such a young age. A sixth grader should never feel like they should end their life, but I did. I'd had enough! I was done with being bullied, I was done with having surgeries, and I was done with failing all my classes. I literally would sit and do hours and hours of homework a night and not understand any of it. I was just done with everything.

It was a Friday afternoon and my mom and I were driving through McDonald's for our weekly ice cream cone. As we were sitting in line, she said, "What would you think if we started a school for you?" All I could think was, *Wow, really?? A school just for me? But wait, wouldn't that just be called homeschooling?* Little did I know, she and my grandma would put their minds together to create something that has literally changed the trajectory of not only my life, but many others as well. My grandma always says, "Where there is a will, there's a way!" Wow, was she right!

The Academy of Saint Louis has been around for 18 years now. It is a school specifically for children with learning differences; from learning disabilities to behavioral problems, this school has helped so many students over the years. While I was at the Academy of Saint Louis, they taught me who I really was and that it is okay to have a disability; there is always a way to learn something even if it's a little differently than everyone else. I thrived there. I was there from sixth grade to twelfth grade when I graduated. I was finally free to be who I really was. This was a big stepping stone into healing from the trauma of being bullied into the person I was meant to be.

Now, back to the moment that changed my life forever. Six minutes into being on Tinder, Jon messaged me. We hit it off right away, and messaged back and forth all night. We learned a lot about each other, including that he has two sons who live with him almost full time. A thought came to me: *Ugh, I told myself I would never date someone with kids! What should I do? This guy is really interesting but he has kids.* I decided not to put too much thought into it since we just started talking. I just couldn't get enough of him. We talked for a couple more days, then decided it would be fun to meet in person!

We planned a date, but he lived about 45 minutes from me. When I go on a first date with a guy I meet on dating sites, I always like to go somewhere that I am familiar with, you know, just in case he is a creeper or something. So, I made him drive closer to where I live. Our plan was to go to lunch and that was it. I like to make short and simple plans for the first date just in case it doesn't go well; I don't want to commit to too much time. We sat at this burger restaurant for hours talking and getting to know each other. Then, we both decided we wanted to hang out longer, so we went down the street to the movie theater and saw a movie. We saw *"Bohemian Rhapsody."* It was a really good movie and I was happy to be getting to spend more time with Jon.

That date was on November 17th, 2018 and was the day that I found my forever person.

So, if you can picture just for a moment what I was going through. I had an apartment with my ex-boyfriend, then my entire apartment was soaked and for weeks all my belongings were wet and damaged, but now I have to tell this wonderful guy I just met about all of this. He never judged me for a second, though. He stepped right in and helped me move to a new apartment. This whole situation really showed me what type of person Jon is. He is there to help you, no matter the situation, because he is a natural helper. Even when he had to face my ex-boyfriend a couple times, he just stayed focused on getting me into a better living situation.

A little later, I found out that he was also in the middle of a weird living situation. Just months before Jon and I met, he helped his mom out of her narcissistic marriage of 30+ years. Jon's mom, along with his brother and sister and their two dogs, moved in with him. There he was, helping two people get away from narcissists at the same time. On Thanksgiving, I went over to his house and got to meet his family. The moment I met his two sons, I didn't care about how I told myself I would never date someone with kids. These two boys are the most amazing kids in the world and I am so thrilled to have them in my life!

A month into our relationship, I ended up in the psych ward for the eighth time. It was a terrifying time for me because I just knew that I would scare Jon away. There was just no way that he was going to stick around after this. He proved me wrong and came to visit me every single day. I was in for 15 days and I have not been back since!

So, what does any of this have to do with self-love? My life before Jon was so dramatic. It seemed like it was just one thing after the other with my physical and mental health. Now, don't get me wrong, I didn't hate my life. I had the most amazing family. My parents have always been nothing but supportive. They would do anything for me. My two siblings also have been two of my biggest supporters. My self-esteem and self-love issues had nothing to do with my home life. In fact, my family were my only safe people in all of my childhood.

My health didn't just magically get better when I met Jon. In fact, I had the biggest surgery of my life a year and a half ago. During the Covid-19 pandemic, I needed brain surgery. Jon drove over an hour to come stay with me. The visiting rules were a little strange since it was Covid, but he was there any chance he could be.

Before meeting Jon there was a huge piece missing in my puzzle. I had never dated a guy who was selfless. Jon was different; he's never made me feel like I was a burden on him because of my health. In the past, I always had to hide my feelings and thoughts because I was worried of scaring whomever I was dating away. With Jon, I knew that I could be me and that was enough for him.

Four years ago, I started to really love myself. I was in an environment that I could thrive in, I had supportive friends and family in my life, and I was taking care of my mental health by continuing to see a therapist and taking my medications on a daily basis. Yet I still felt like a crucial part was missing and didn't know where I belonged in the world. I still was very unclear about my purpose on the planet. For the first three years of my relationship with Jon, I still struggled with depression. I loved myself, but just in the "I don't hate myself anymore" kind of way. Then, on July 30th, 2022, everything fell in alignment and I could finally say for the first time ever that I am living my best life.

I met a lady through a mutual friend. I had been Facebook friends with her for some time but we never really talked, and I hadn't really paid attention to the content on her profile. She was just another one of my 3,500 friends. Well, one day I decided to look into her and I am so happy that I did. She is a high-performance business coach and she is also a psychologist. She was talking about this program she created called Ascente. She and I talked about the program and I fell in love with the concept. I just ***had*** to be in this program, so I signed up. During one of the Zoom calls, she mentioned that her client concierge was quitting. I reached out to her to inquire about what being a client concierge entailed. I messaged her and said, "Dr. Erin, I think I would be so good at being your client concierge." She agreed! I had never felt the kind of excitement that I did that day.

Ever since I was in grade school, I had always wanted to be a therapist. I am a fantastic listener and I am really good at problem solving. Once I realized what schooling I would have to go through to achieve that dream, I knew that wasn't going to happen. "If only therapists needed assistants," I told myself for years. Well, my dream came true! I get to be an assistant to a therapist! Sure, she's not in practice as a mental health therapist at the moment, and a client concierge is basically a fancy name for an assistant, but I'm doing what I had wished for and that's all that matters.

I have learned what true friendship means by being in her world. Friendship is something I always lacked in my life. She showed me what it means to be a human being with all the emotions. She's taught me that no emotion is bad; it just is what it is. She showed me it's okay to cry, it's okay to be upset, and how empowering it is to share your accomplishments with those around you. One of the most exciting things I have learned by being her client concierge is that I have a purpose on this planet, and that purpose is to help her with her life's mission —to set the captives free! If I can help her become a millionaire in the meantime, that's a plus!

She told me from day one that her purpose on the planet is to set the captives free. I wondered what that meant, but now I understand! Before joining her team at "The Higher Life," I led a mundane existence. I didn't hate life, but I didn't love it either. It just was what it was. I had a routine and I loved the people I got to share my daily life with, but it was dull. I didn't know achieving a different, happier life was possible. She set me free! I was captive in my own body. I was lifeless and grasped at whatever exciting thing was going on that day, unaware of what I was meant to do. Now I am free and loving every moment of my life with my fiancé, his two amazing boys, and waking up every morning ready to take on the world with a new-found fire in my soul.

So, if you're keeping track, I have finally conquered all three steps to self-love! I am living in an environment that builds me up with the greatest family and friends. I have been working daily on my mental health with all the skills my therapist has helped me with over the last eight years, and I have a purpose on the planet that lights me up more than anything ever has in my lifetime!

Lessons Learned:

1. Be selective with who you let into your circle of importance and who you spend your time with.
2. Speak up; always advocate for yourself.
3. Don't be afraid to change your situation for fear of what is next.

Mindset Tips:

1. Find a mental health therapist. Every single person on this planet can benefit from seeing one.
2. Do self-care every day. This could be meditating, reading, or just spending a few minutes with yourself. Just do something for yourself every single day.
3. Find your purpose on the planet!

Aha Moments and Self-Reflections

Note your Thoughts

Krista Enslow

Krista Enslow, born and raised in Nova Scotia, now resides on Vancouver Island, British Columbia with her partner and 10-year-old daughter. She is an entrepreneur in financial education who recruits and trains leaders while helping families ease the burden of financial stress. Krista enjoys rescuing animals and is a hobby farmer with over 30 chickens, nine ducks, and nine rabbits. She loves hikes and foraging for berries, plants, and mushrooms, doing cold dips, having coffee on the porch, and evenings with a big bowl of popcorn. Personal development is her love language as well as spiritualism. She is always seeking out connections in life, to people, plants, and animals. She is a truth seeker and expert BS detector. This is Krista's first time writing a chapter in a book, and she chose this one because her recent connection to self-love is an experience she wanted to share.

Connect with Krista:

https://www.linkedin.com/in/krista-enslow/
https://www.instagram.com/Kristathek/
https://agents.wfgcanada.ca/krista-enslow

Chapter 12

Self-Love Creates Success

By Krista Enslow

A friend of mine posted a meme on Facebook a while ago, and it has been coming up in my mind daily ever since. The meme says, "If I asked you to name all the things you love, how long would it take you to name yourself?" That really stopped me in my tracks. I was awake for days sorting through feeling after feeling and wondering if I had any self-love. "Well, of course, I have self-love!" I declared aloud. Why did I hesitate? What was that hesitation about? Now I am down the rabbit hole of what self-love has to do with anything I say and do. So, what has self-love got to do with it? I believe that it has everything to do with it.

Being an entrepreneur, especially in the finance industry, you must truly love to help people. You have to feel that deep inside of yourself, you deserve as great a life as the one you are planning for your clients and teammates. As well, in order to help so many people get the financial education they rightfully deserve, you NEED to show them what can be done despite their limiting beliefs; one must pour into them, show them their futures, put them in the place they want to be in their minds, and must not take no for an answer. You are their conduit for every dream and goal they have, and to convey that realistically, you have to believe in yourself and them, as well as have the integrity and conviction to relay your emotion behind why you do what you do and why you want to get to know them on a personal level. For all of this to fall into place like one would want, you need to start with yourself and look within. Personal development at its finest is working inside out, and being clear with yourself to know what you really want. This is how it all comes into play; the big picture is all about self-love.

Self-love is a learned behavior. We aren't born knowing how to take care of ourselves, in any aspect, especially spiritually. It can be exceedingly difficult, especially for folks who come from trauma, or even a full and rich family unit, if the disconnect between external and internal love is there. Can we even fully love others if we are not in love with ourselves first? How do we learn this, and where does it come from? Is there a step-by-step instruction guide in our life manuals? (Wouldn't it be nice to have one of those? Ha-ha!) This journey is ongoing.

I didn't just wake up one morning and say, "Okay Krista, today is the day to love yourself" and have it be so. I tried that and it didn't work. The reason I know it didn't work is that when I looked at my past and thought about the things that I considered a good idea at the time, knowing what I know now, I can definitely say that I did NOT love myself. Heck, I didn't even like myself, which was evident by the people that I let define me, control me, and tell me I was great. I let myself be loved based on what people told me I was and what I could be, and not based on any self-love foundation. It was beyond clear that I had ZERO ideas of what self-love was. I was not living my best life and was not truly happy, at least not the type of happiness a person gets when they are on a self-discovery journey, and they have the light bulb go off. I was quite the opposite, and it wasn't until I was just about 40 that I realized I am in control of how I felt about myself and that only I can change how I feel about myself. This is where the twisty, bumpy road of personal development began. When I look back on my 30s and the personal development I tried to do, it's not anything like what I'm doing now or for the past couple of years.

For as long as I can remember, I always wanted people to like me, and to think of me first before anyone else, so I would do just about anything that was asked of me, and more, at school, my jobs, and even at home. I wanted to be known and I wanted to be in first place for everything, and for no other reason than to have people like me and remember me. I craved it daily so I could feel good. I was making everyone happy and honestly believed that was how I was supposed to be. I lived like this my entire life. Looking outward for my self-esteem and self-love.

In high school, I always picked friends with parental problems or any kind of problem so I could bring them home to "fix them" in the hopes that they would like me and think of me as the "helpful person." Once I knew I was helping them, I would get that wonderful feeling of self-love again. I would have boyfriends in high school with a high caliber of baggage and I would do my best to fix them all so that they would like me and then I could be happy. I constantly wanted everyone to know I was there for them and would do anything for them, all so that I could have that feeling. At the time, I had NO idea I was craving that feeling or even understood what I was doing.

My grade 12 relationship was with a guy whose father killed himself. When we got involved, it hadn't even been a full year since he lost his dad, and he was angry. He was also new to being in a relationship, and he told me he didn't know what to do in one or how it should be. I still remember that conversation to this day, and how we both spent the better part of seven years trying to figure each other out and despite breaking up countless times, we always found a way back to each other. It wasn't until we were near 30 years old that we realized we could be best friends, but nothing more. At one point, we didn't talk for over a year, but I still knew that of all the humans on this earth, he would always be my constant. It was also right around this time that I started to realize that maybe I might be responsible for my own feelings and that I also might be responsible for how I perceive feelings from others; that it was on me if I felt triggered by someone else's feelings. During one of our break-ups, I tried to date, but that turned out to be a nightmare because I was still looking for someone to help in some way. When I couldn't find someone who needed it, I would try to help other guy friends with any worry in the world that they had, but sometimes that turned out not to be what I thought it was; they were after something else and I was craving a feeling that I didn't know I was after. My mid-20s were interesting, that's for sure.

I had a relationship long after that one had ended, and it was an absolute train wreck. I didn't see that while I was in it, but it really was. It was full of manipulation and narcissism; he was also snorting cocaine on occasion, and emotional abuse was a daily occurrence. I was doing whatever I could to make him like me so that I could be ok with myself, all while running our restaurant and doing anything I could to make the staff like him. When I was the reason that the staff listened, I could carry on having all the self-esteem and love in the world. Even after he cheated on me many times, and confirmed this himself, I spent almost four months doing whatever he wanted so that he would still like me, and I could continue to have the self-love that I never wanted to lose. I could write an entire book about this portion of my life. I spent nearly six years in counseling to deal with the years of 2010 and 2011, and yet, subconsciously, I still believed that my self-love was because of all these people in my life, abuse and all.

The relationship didn't end well, He stalked and harassed me, my parents, and my current partner for months. It was awful. At the time, I had no idea what was really happening, and could not even think about taking care of myself because I was too busy being pregnant with my daughter, whose father is my current partner, and helping to get him and his kids situated in a new town. Once again, in a helping situation, I was subconsciously following a feeling and thrown from one fire into another, only this one was a slow burn. It's now 11 years into my current relationship. We have a daughter and I have two stepchildren who are adults. I've never been fully welcomed as a stepmother; I have spent the entire duration of this part of my life "people pleasing," just like times before. I always seem to find someone to "fix" or "repair," all the while being absolutely miserable in my own house, yet honestly believing that what I was doing was okay, because that's what I had to do. You make your bed and now lie in it, right?

In February 2020, my friend, Carol, came by my house and introduced me to the company that I currently work with. (I don't work *for* them; I am an independent broker as they are the brokerage house). I thought she was crazy and when she brought me to the office for team training, I was convinced that everyone there needed some serious medication. It was a room filled with super happy people, not only talking about their goals and dreams, but making them a reality, and that just made zero sense to me. I was sure I knew that it was fine to say things out loud, but my previous dreams and goals had been squashed so many times that there was no way this new career of mine could possibly bring any hope back. I was there to support Carol and nothing else. But when I heard I had to study for some tests that I needed to take to get paid legally, I wasn't sure I could stay. TESTS! That was it, I was out! At least I thought I was. Then in March of the same year, Covid-19 put a halt on everyone's lives. The licensing branch had closed the testing centers, which meant there wasn't any way for me to take the provincial tests. I was saved by the pandemic and had nearly an entire year of being unlicensed in the finance sector, so I was along for the ride. What else was I doing? Nothing. Everything was closed.

Every training had a part of personal development with it, and I soon started to understand through all these leaders that for any business to thrive, one must be okay with themself. There are so many levels of being okay with yourself that it's almost impossible to nail down just one thing at a time. I remember an exercise we did, and the point was to figure out your worth. I couldn't even get the first part done without bursting into tears. I had no idea what my worth was and trying to figure it out was the hardest thing I had done in a long time. I couldn't understand why that was so difficult for me. I had spent my life having what I thought were feelings of self-love encompass my entire being. Then, I found myself doing personal development and realized it had nothing to do with anyone other than myself, and had everything to do with looking within, having my own feelings and emotions, being accountable, and understanding who I am at my very core. There was no one to repair on my team, and nobody to get my feelings from; everyone was supportive and wanted me to be the best version of myself for me and my family. This was so foreign to me that it might as well be written in alien hieroglyphs. Nonetheless, with each week that I stayed involved and learned from everyone, I was moving ahead in business and growing personally, though I had no idea it was happening. Finally, the industry pivoted and by November, I was writing my provincials in Victoria and submitting paperwork to the Insurance Council, all while learning about how to be the best leader and teammate. Who knew being an effective entrepreneur meant knowing more about yourself than you'd like to know?

By the beginning of 2021, I was no longer looking for others to give me a feeling of worthiness, and I was well on my way to understanding that everything we need comes from within. I was learning that unless we are on a mission to better our love for ourselves and feel what is there, how can we expect others to want to be around us or follow us? "Would you follow you?" is a question that comes up almost every day on our team. We are all entrepreneurs here and we all work together every day to lift each other up. Who knew that finance would be such a self-discovery journey? Helping clients from all social classes succeed in their goals and dreams can only happen if you are in love with yourself and what you are doing. Having people be part of your team and trust you when they have no trust in themselves, can only happen when you have the belief and are truly connecting with yourself, as well as when you're surrounding yourself with positive people who are crushing their goals and dreaming big, all while helping families financially. Every partner in this firm pouring into us daily about the importance of self-empowerment makes me feel stronger and more confident each day in every aspect of my business. The personal development game is so fluid that you don't realize you are doing it until you hit some tough obstacles and you have choices to make.

Discovering true self-love can sometimes come with some anger and tears. Digging deep within yourself shows you what you are truly made of. Confidence and happiness are a by-product of all your hard work. Unfortunately, some people will get left behind. There will be people who are not going to be with you on your path. It's not that we are outgrowing them, but rather we are raising our personal vibration, and our old self is being reborn into a new version of being. We are now only resonating with those who inspire and vibrate with us. Some people will not be excited about your growth, and you will notice that you are not talking to them as much or wanting to spend time with them. This is normal. I have learned that personal development is not about other people; it's about you and growing up. We are the solution; we are all we need. In saying that, though, we can also be the problem without the proper tools.

I've been finding that the road to self-love is never-ending. It will never be fully found because it's not supposed to be found. It's designed for us to always be working on ourselves and for us to always be alert and grounded; to be present and know what we want and to work towards it; to find people to be on the journey with who will truly be there for us. The truth of it is that you cannot fully support anyone else unless you are taking care of yourself. You may have friends or family in your life who have no idea what you are doing, or why "you've changed," and that's okay. They can tell you what they think, and they can throw all the negativity of the world your way. People are going to be uncomfortable with the new you. They will not have any understanding of your growth because it is your personal journey, and they may not be there yet. Also, they may NEVER get there, so prepare for that as well. We've done nothing wrong in learning to love ourselves and working out the kinks in our previous life map.

It's a little funny when you think about running a business and building a strong team, that your mind goes to everything BUT personal development. Other questions may go through your mind—*How much money do I need for the month? How much goes to savings? How can I get everyone on training appointments? Who is making supper? What about the kids?* —and the fact is when you let everything you've learned about yourself marinate, all those questions are answered, and your business is the easiest part of your day! A business is only as strong as we are. Without our heart in it, and without our heart guiding every decision we make, the business will not be an easy road. Self-love is first and foremost, and I love that it will never be an end game for me. It's uncomfortable as hell, yet the most rewarding thing I've ever done. No more looking outside for my feelings; no more listening to others who have no idea how I feel or how I should feel. I do not even ask for advice from anyone, especially because now I know that not everyone is the same, and another person's outlook on my life will not benefit me at all.

We all have the potential to be amazing humans. Every human has a drive and passion, though many haven't found it yet. That is their journey and this is mine. Self-love and self-worth are the foundation of all the strength I need to crush every goal I have, and it allows me to dream again. I have the freedom to be happy in my own skin, and the freedom to allow certain people into my life as I see fit. I have the freedom and confidence to express who I am in a positive way and bring light into a darkened room. This road isn't paved, and it's filled with mud and holes, but I can see through the obstacles because my eyes are opened; I spend time in meditation and watching good content online. And by good content, I mean videos that teach you something to use in your daily life to be a better person, a better parent, a better partner, or a better entrepreneur. Or sign up for podcasts and seminars that personal development gurus like Tony Robbins or Ed Mylett host.

There was no pivotal moment in which I knew change was needed. Each part of my life's journey brings individual moments that require attention. I am an entirely different person today than I was two years ago, two months ago, and even two weeks ago. I know that self-love will be a new daily habit and a positive one. I will build myself while building leaders, and I will continue to strive to be a better version of myself so that I can show others how to build themselves up. If someone doesn't want to get on the wagon, then they don't have to. I will still send them love and light; never a judgment or a harsh word. I am just enjoying my soul and heart so much right now that it frightens me to damage them, so I have decided to never stop self-loving. I will never stop being positive or stop being relatable to anyone and that is because I am finally working on ME and climbing every day to catch a glimpse of my full potential. If your business or home life isn't where it should be, look inside yourself. You are the solution to all your worries. Let go of the fear of losing because success is just on the other side.

My Life Lessons:

1. Don't look behind you; you aren't going that way.
2. Be the lighthouse always, no matter what.
3. Your brain will always protect the body, not the soul—that's what your heart is for.

My Mindset Tips:

1. Meditate: Calming the mind and body to allow proper breathing is **essential** to long-term overall health.
2. Find at least 5 things every day to be grateful for, even when you think you're having the worst time. There's always something to be grateful for. Dig deep and find it.
3. Get away from negative, toxic people—those who complain constantly, or are everyday victims; the ones who will do nothing to change their lives; those who are not willing to personally grow and become better—doesn't matter if they're family or your best friend. They will suck the life out of you.

Aha Moments and Self-Reflections

Note your Thoughts

Melinda Pokolinski

Daughter, wife, mother, teacher, writer, and birthmother. Melinda Pokolinski is all of these things and more. Her vision is to share her experience and journey as a birthmother to improve how society perceives open adoption. Melinda's mission is to help increase the number of successful, happy, open adoptions. She has experiences and strategies to share that emphasize self-love and knowing yourself to follow God's purpose in your life. This self-love, which was built through a strong and loving support system (her bottom hands) throughout her life, is what allows her to pass these practices on to her students in the classroom and on to society as an open adoption advocate. Melinda uses what has been shown to her about a loving family to build her own loving family with her husband and son. Through time, reflection, bravery, prayer, pondering, therapy, and all the things, Melinda has learned to love and accept who she is with compassion and pride and, ultimately, that she is a bottom hand. Melinda knows that she was led through these experiences to help others and support them with all the love and support she was given to follow God's plan and purpose for life. This chapter is a stepping stone to her book, *Divine Option*, about her open adoption journey and how to make it a positive experience for everyone involved.

Connect with Melinda:

https://www.divineoptionstory.com/
https://www.facebook.com/divineoptionstory
https://linktr.ee/melindacolette

Chapter 13

Beautifully Broken

By Melinda Pokolinski

And we know that God causes everything to work together for the good of those who love God and are called according to His purpose for them. Romans 8:28 (NLT)

Have you ever felt like you had a particular purpose in life? As if you had a specific role to fulfill, but it didn't make itself clear until a certain moment? And because of all the broken and beautiful parts of who you are, you are the only person who can fulfill that role? I have, and I do; her name is Grace. It's not to say I don't have other purposes in life; I have many beautiful, important roles to fulfill. I believe in all of them, and I am grateful for all of them. But Grace was a divine purpose I didn't know I had until she happened. While this is a story of open adoption, it is also a narrative of bottom hands, the beautifully broken, and the value of self-love. This divine journey led to my understanding of why I am who I am, why God created me this way and chose me to help fulfill His plan. This journey is ongoing, but what has been revealed over time is why even our broken pieces are precious and essential in God's plan.

When I was 29, I was in university studying to become a teacher. I was enjoying my life and happy to have found a purpose in teaching, but I was lonely and yearning for a loving relationship. I wanted to meet a guy who truly loved me and knew all of me—the broken and the beautiful—and wanted to build and share a life with me; someone who would be a safe place for me even though I was beautifully broken. I had a good friend who was so fun to flirt with, talk to, and dance with, and we had a wonderful history that warms my heart to this day. We truly enjoyed and loved each other as friends, and one night, we were at the same club, and we decided to return to his place together. We both had enough to drink that our inhibitions were gone, and we had thrown caution to the wind. Being with someone who cared about me was what I needed at the time. I wanted to feel beautiful and loved, and to believe that it was exactly what I wanted and needed.

As I walked home after that intimate night with my friend, I knew deep inside that a powerful and divine journey had started; something within me reminded me that I had a purpose, even though I knew that what I had just done was not the best choice. It was a choice that a broken part of me had made. It was a temptation that I wasn't strong enough to evade.

Six weeks later, a second pregnancy test confirmed my suspicions: I was expecting a baby, and I didn't know what I was going to do. I sat on the floor of my living room while I cried, prayed, laughed, and shook my head in disbelief and wonder. I pondered what all of this meant and why I had let it happen. I beat myself up and said nasty things to myself. I honestly thought I only had two options: I was either going to raise the baby by myself, or I was going to have an abortion. And somewhere along the way, I miraculously fell in love with someone I didn't even know—my baby.

Only after a beautiful visit with a friend, whom I consider a bottom hand (someone who is a safe place to land, an encourager and someone who loves you unconditionally), did I come to a realization that I hadn't considered. This friend made me understand that very often when you think you only have two choices, there is usually a third option that you have overlooked. For me, this third option was open adoption. Once this possibility was placed in front of me, the option that turned my stomach and I knew I could not live with, disappeared instantly. I still wasn't sure if I would keep and raise my baby or gift my baby to another family for adoption, but I was thankful that the choices I now had before me were both something I could live with. I was certain one choice wasn't easier than the other, and that they were just very different. I remember hearing God's warm, loving voice inside me say, "You'll know when you need to know." After serious prayer, reflection, discussion with bottom hands, and education, I waited for an answer.

It was when I was talking with the father of my baby (still a dear friend) that I suddenly knew that the best choice for *me*, and God's will, was that I gift this baby to an amazing family. This revelation filled me with peace, and it was divine; it was God's mercy for a choice I wouldn't have made if I wasn't beautifully broken. Grace is defined as divine mercy, and that is exactly who this precious girl was and is for me to this day.

When those big plans began to take form, I knew she was part of my purpose. Every part of me, the broken and the beautiful, brought my purpose to life. Grace was my divine mercy and showed me that we are all beautifully flawed for His purpose and plan. The broken pieces were a part of me, and as I fixed or worked with them, loved them, and accepted them, I became more beautiful and accepting of myself and others. As I followed God's will and trusted the peace He sent me, I knew that the choices I made because of who I was would allow me to show His mercy and His work in my life. All the things that I was learning along this journey were things that I would be able to share with others. In 2 Corinthians 1:4, it says, "He comforts us in all our troubles so that we can comfort others. When they are troubled, we will be able to give them the same comfort God has given us." There is so much value in having something important to share with the world. If we don't love or have compassion for ourselves, though, then we are not going to be able to fulfill God's will, nor be able to take what we've learned and experienced to help others.

I believe my conviction in this decision to gift my baby girl in an open adoption came from my sincere sense of self-worth. As a young adult, I sometimes wondered where my self-esteem came from. I was never the most popular, the prettiest, or the smartest. I was happy, though; I knew what mattered, and I knew who mattered. I knew who I was, and I could tell myself the truth. If someone was nasty to me or didn't want to be friends, it was like water off a duck's back for me. I had my people; I didn't need people in my world who didn't appreciate or accept who I was. I knew I wasn't perfect; I was broken and beautiful, and that is who I was supposed to be. At some level, I always knew that there were big plans for me, but I just wasn't sure what they were… yet.

How did I know all those things that I needed to love about myself? Because the people in my world shared those things with me. Dr. Jody Carrington refers to such precious people as your "bottom hands, your safe place to land." Whenever I was unsure of myself or wasn't "feelin' the (self) love," I could always seek solace in my safe place and with my people. If you had asked me where my favourite place to be was when I was young, I would have told you that it was the living room in my home or my grandparent's home.

My maternal grandparents gifted the world with nine magnificent children, but more importantly, they gifted them with the knowledge of how to be a part of a loving, supportive family. I was blessed to have my cousins as my best friends and my parents, brother, grandparents, aunts and uncles there to love and cheer me on. Gramma would place her hands on my face and look deep into my eyes and say, "I love you, Melinda, you are so beautiful," in her beautiful soft voice and strong French-Canadian accent, and I would melt. I still do when I think about it, and it fills my heart with such love. Gramma made me feel like I was the only person who mattered to her on the planet! There was nothing I could do that would ever shatter her love for me, and she passed that ability on to my mom because my mom still makes me feel the same way. Even the broken parts of me that I would rather sweep under a rug would never be enough to shake their faith in my worth. Those two ladies taught me that every part of me mattered. Their faith and love are a constant reminder to me that God loves you no matter what.

One of the beautiful (and practical) things my mom and I did when I was a pre-teen was to write letters and notes to each other. I have to say, I was a very mean pre-teen to my mom, and I am sure that I hurt her many times with the unkind, thoughtless things I would say. Thus, the letters became a way for us to slow down, and to communicate without getting mad at each other. We might agree to disagree, but Mom would always end those letters with "God loves you! Jesus loves you! And so do I!"

This always made me believe I had a purpose—even the broken parts of me were important. I didn't know my purpose at a young age, but I knew I was being prepared for something significant and divine. Our brokenness often pushes us to selfish decisions that we truly believe are acceptable at the time. The choice I made was to be physically intimate with a good friend. I believed we both wanted and needed that intimacy. Remarkably, it was that choice that brought about the journey that taught me everything we do will be used to give glory to God if we love Him.

There are so many things that God caused to work together for the good in my life, but what has had the greatest impact on me is my bottom hands. If I did not have the love and support that they continue to show me, I would spend so much energy on the negative notions and the broken pieces that I would never remember who I truly am. Most of the time, I know who I am, and I have purpose in life, but like everyone else, it escapes me at times, and I just don't love (or even like) myself very much. This happens especially when things are not going as planned, or life seems to be spinning out of control, and I am too tired, or I don't want to be doing what I'm doing, and so on. I start turning on myself sometimes, and a lot of times, all the self-care (bubble baths, walks, meditation, naps) in the world doesn't make me feel better. What does change those nasty thoughts is telling myself the truth, falling into the people who love me (my bottom hands), and reminding myself of what I know about who I am and why I am on this beautifully broken planet that I live on. My mom reminds me of the people in her world who have shared with her what a special person I am. I am blessed with beautiful women in my life who I call my "other mothers." Two of my mom's best friends remind me that I live a good life and have so much to offer; they make me feel so special and loved. The mom of one of my best friends treats me like I am one of her daughters, and she loves them so well!

But it is not only women who are my bottom hands. I have been incredibly blessed in my life—I met the man to whom I am married, and we have a wonderful life beyond what I ever imagined. Ken and I are like an intricate puzzle with different size pieces that all fit together in the most incredible ways. He has become my most beloved and cherished bottom hand, and I think it is safe to say that I have become his. Our marriage and our friendship are a constant that I never want to live without. Our son, Andrew, joined us in 2011, and Ken and I have grown together as his bottom hands. We work hard to love each other well and ensure that we all know unconditional love and acceptance.

Working together and supporting each other as a team is what I always imagined my family to look like. It is also one of the biggest reasons I gifted Grace to her family. I wanted to give her what I loved about my family; my mom and dad always there to guide me and assure me that I mattered, I was loved, and God had plans for me. I chose a family for her that was just like the one I grew up with—one with the same values and love for each other. Being connected to each other and caring for each other is what makes relationships safe, loving, and healthy. I learned that from my family, and I carry that on with my own. I would never have gifted my baby if I couldn't have an honest, open relationship with her and her parents. The relationships I have in my life were proof to me that I was loved and accepted unconditionally, and because of their faith in me, I was able to move forward and choose the best family for my baby, I was certain that she was going to grow up with the same—and she has.

These relationships with my bottom hands serve to remind me of what I already know and love about myself. I matter to these people, and they matter to me. What I have learned, though, is that if I am not okay, if I am not caring for and loving myself, then I am less able to support and love those around me. In 2017, when I started following and listening to Dr. Jody Carrington, one phrase particularly resonated with me, as a teacher. She said, "If our teachers are not okay, our babies don't stand a chance."

I believe that a way to experience self-love is to stand back and try to see yourself as others see you and to treat yourself as they would treat you. That's why we must believe what our bottom hands tell us about ourselves! They see things about us that we don't always see. They remind us of who we are when we forget! How many parents tell their children, "If you could only see yourself the way I see you!" It is so true; your bottom hands are the ones who know and love you better than anyone else on earth. Self-love is a reflection of their approbation and admiration. When someone has lost their way and doesn't know who their bottom hands are, they must search to find those people because they are there—and they are precious. Without them, we don't have anyone to remind us of who we are at our beautifully broken core.

Making all of our self-love puzzle pieces fit together takes hard work. It is nothing less than a roller coaster ride. All the emotions—physical and psychological—fear, exhilaration, stomach-in-your-throat, hands in the air, and questioning why you did something, are all feelings we have when we are learning who we truly are and who we are supposed to be in God's purpose and plan. It takes time, reflection, bravery, prayer, pondering, therapy, and all the things to love and accept who we are with compassion and pride. Truth be told, as I have learned to have more compassion for myself and all the choices I make, I have become more compassionate toward others and their choices. I have empathy for people learning from their choices. I want to help people see their beauty because I have learned through experience what it means to see, accept, and appreciate mine. I have chosen to see my beauty and believe in what I know to be true about myself. In doing so, I have become a bottom hand who is able to support my friends and family when they have self-doubts.

We must focus on what we know to be true and choose joy. Jessica Janzen, in her book, *Bring the Joy*, talks about how even when times are harder-than-hard and you are feeling life is impossible, you should choose to find joy, dance through the hard times, and embrace the lessons you can learn about life and yourself. When you spend your energy on the positive side instead of the negative, beautiful things will happen. We bring about what we spend time thinking about!

Even when I was making things hard for my mom, when I was saying hurtful, disrespectful things, she focused on the things she loved about me, and she shared those things with me. As my number one bottom hand, she loved on me unconditionally, and she made that her choice. We must make that choice for ourselves, too. Mel Robbins says, "Your superpower is that there is only one you." I believe with all my heart that is what God depends on, too; there is only one me, and there is only one you. We are a part of God's purpose and plan, and He uses the broken choices we make to fulfill His plan.

We are who we are for a reason, and life would not be the same without us. What a treasure we are to the world! My self-care is taking care of that treasure by enjoying every second I have on this beautifully broken planet I live on with the people I love, my bottom hands. If I'm not okay, then my people are not okay. A good friend of mine, a bottom hand, shared with me that taking care of and being with my people is a big part of my self-love, and she is so right! She reminds me every time I'm going through tough stuff that I have to accept challenges with grace and decide what I am supposed to be learning from it. How can I make it an opportunity for me to create a better version of myself? What a vicious cycle it would become if we never learned to love the broken and the beautiful about ourselves, or to appreciate what this knowledge can offer others!

What is the next step for me? I have plans to write a book about my open adoption journey. Do I think I can do it? Not yet. The broken part would say "never," but the "not yet" is the important and beautiful part. I'm getting there. There is so much learning to do; I have to be kind to myself in the process, and I have to remember the beautiful things about me that are going to get this book written. I am taking the steps, but I'm not there yet, and that is okay because I have my bottom hands, and with them, I will get there.

The opportunity to write a chapter for this book is a step in the right direction. It makes me happy when I can share my experiences with others. It gives me reason and purpose.

Helping others learn how to enhance their self-love gives me joy. It makes me sad to see people just smile and nod when a compliment is shared with them. I want to help people learn to accept and believe in those compliments, especially when the praises come from their bottom hands. We have so much to learn in this beautiful life, so why not learn it everywhere we can? We are all works in progress, and when we take on an attitude of joy and compassion, we can fully accept and appreciate how beautifully broken we are. It allows us to be kind to ourselves and those around us. Using our beauty as a gift and working on the broken will continue to make us more into who we are supposed to be.

Surround yourself with people who know, love, and accept you. Surround yourself with people who will be real and compassionate with you. As Dr. Jody says, "Sit with the winners—the conversation is different." The people who matter will remind you why you matter and who you truly are; believe them, spend time with them, let them love on you, and love on them. Through the most challenging and emotional times in my open adoption journey, I sat with my people as much as I could. My parents supported me in the most selfless ways. They would have been struggling, too. My family and my friends, my bottom hands, had my back, even if they didn't understand the choice I was making. They were real, and they were compassionate! They reminded me of who I was and what my purpose was. These are the things that enhance my self-love. These are the things that remind me of my purpose. These things help me choose joy and hope, and trust in my bottom hands and God's purpose and plan for me. These are the gifts that I want to share—for I now understand the value of the beautifully broken, the role of bottom hands, and the need for self-love.

Lessons Learned:

1. Every part of who we are—good, broken and beautiful—sets us apart for a divine purpose.
2. When you are compassionate with yourself and love all parts of you, your divine purpose is revealed and fulfilled because YOU are the only one who can be in that role.
3. Without my bottom hands, I would not have made the choices I did in my life. They know me and love me, and that led me to my divine purpose.

Mindset Tips:

1. Tell yourself the truth. You are broken and beautiful so that you can fulfill God's purpose.
2. You are not alone on this journey. Fall into your people. The path you are meant to follow will be revealed, through time and your bottom hands. When you are low on self-love, allow your people, your bottom hands, to remind you who you are, what your purpose is, and why you are loved.
3. Your self-love journey is just that, a journey. There will be hills and valleys and rabbit holes. Allow yourself to live, love, and learn along the path. Be compassionate and loving to yourself through the journey.

Aha Moments and Self-Reflections

Note your Thoughts

Reena Yost

Reena Yost was born and raised in Edmonton, Alberta. She grew up in the foster care system and moved in and out of 8-9 foster homes and one group home before she turned 16. She developed a very strong bond with her two siblings who were with her through parts of her journey. Reena found her faith at a young age and always knew she was destined for more. Starting self-love and mindset practices in her early adulthood, she has overcome many lessons and is grateful for the blessings that came from them. Reena now lives in beautiful Kelowna, British Columbia with her amazing 16-year-old daughter and her supportive and loving boyfriend. She has been a licensed REALTOR® in Edmonton since 2006 and still has her business in operation there. Reena also is the owner of Alchemy Real Estate Group and runs her real estate team out of RE/MAX Kelowna. This year, Reena, along with a partner and friend, started a renovation and design business called Oak & Onyx Interiors, which serves Kelowna and the Okanagan areas. Reena organizes many charity events and is working on sharing her story on multiple platforms. She has a passion to help children to become mindful and love themselves through all of their lessons. Reena believes awareness is key and the earlier you become aware, the earlier you can learn to love yourself fully.

Connect with Reena:

https://www.facebook.com/AlchemyRealEstateGroup
https://www.instagram.com/real_estate_reena
https://www.linkedin.com/in/reenayost/

Chapter 14

Blessings, Faith, and Love

By Reena Yost

Self-love is a lot of things. It's self-awareness, self-acceptance, accountability, strength, faith, self-compassion, forgiveness, commitment, and gratitude. It is accepting your imperfections, and giving yourself time to breathe. It is knowing that you are important; you're here for a reason and self-love is believing that—it is belief in yourself.

I want to talk about faith.

I didn't learn about God or religion through my family. I went to Catholic school and learned a bit about religion that way, but there were two pivotal moments in my life when I really felt my faith grow.

Firstly, it's important to mention that I only have a portion of my memories from my childhood. I realized that I have blocked out a lot of them, which is quite normal. Children who experience traumatic events or a tough childhood may respond by dissociating or mentally detaching, which could affect how they remember or how much they remember. These memories don't usually disappear completely but they may not fully understand what happened. One of my first memories ever was when I was probably three or four years old. I was living with a foster family who had an acreage. It was my older sister of 10 months, Roxanne, and my younger brother of two and a half years, Ryan, who lived with me as well. I don't remember many details other than they had kittens that lived outside and I accidentally broke one of the kitten's legs, which was traumatizing. I don't even remember that moment; I only remember knowing that was what happened and I think I remember that because of how horrible I felt about it. The other memory of that home was when I was climbing up a treehouse, and there was a nail sticking out that pierced my finger as I was climbing. We had to have someone cut out the piece of wood and bring me to the hospital to have it removed. I've wondered why I only remember two sad moments, but I realized it's because they were traumatic.

I don't remember the transition from that home, or moving back to my biological mom's house, but I do remember my mom wasn't there to take care of us. There was a lady who was called a homemaker—I'm not even sure the details of who she was or if she was sent by social services, but she is a lady I still think of often—her name was Helen. I remember her name so clearly because I thought it was ironic that her name starts with the word "hell," considering she was the first person that told me about God and taught me how to pray. Helen tucked me in at night and talked to me about God. She told me I can ask God anything through prayer and he will answer my prayers. She taught me to kneel beside my bed, close my eyes, and put my hands together palm to palm. She told me to pray the *Our Father* and the *Hail Mary* and then to give thanks and ask God for blessings. I would pray to God to keep me and my family safe, but most of all, my prayers were always for my mom. I prayed that she would get better, stop using drugs and alcohol, and be able to take care of us. I prayed for my mom because all I wanted was to be with her. I don't remember Helen taking care of us for too long, but her teachings have never left me. She contributed to my faith, and I am so grateful for her presence in my life. I hope wherever she is that she knows how much she impacted me and my life.

Shortly after Helen left, my sister and I were in a foster home where the foster parents had two other kids as well. The foster mom treated us like maids. I remember every Saturday we had to clean the entire house, which consisted of a front room with a piano, a lot of crystal items, and furniture. It was a huge house. We had to vacuum, wash floors, clean bathrooms, do all the laundry, including the foster parents and their children's clothes, fold them, and put them away. We did all the bedding in the entire house as well. We had to dust everything, and I mean everything, then they allowed their kids to check if we had done a good job. If they had found a speck of dust on their fingers, we had to do it all over again. The foster mom liked to entertain and it was our job to clean up after everyone left, including washing all the dishes by hand. I listened because I had to. I didn't have a voice or a choice. I felt this was my job; my contribution to be allowed to live there. I knew it wasn't fair that their kids didn't have the same chores, or that they were allowed to treat us that way, but I didn't feel that I had any other options.

Throughout this time, Helen's teachings never wavered. I prayed every single night before bed. I prayed for my siblings. I prayed for our mom to get better so she could take care of us. Through tears, I prayed to have a normal family. I prayed so hard, every day. Then, finally, God answered our prayers. We were able to go home! I was so happy! We all were. I thanked God for answering my prayers. I was so grateful and relieved; my faith grew. I felt God had listened to all my prayers, sadness, and longing to be with my mom.

Unfortunately, it didn't last long. Approximately three to four weeks after we moved back in with her, my mom said we were going to the mall to buy a slip for me. I was excited to buy this silky undergarment to go under my dress, so I put a one-dollar coin that I had in my pocket, and off we went. My mom, sister, brother, and I were walking for a little bit and then came to a big building that looked more like an office than a mall. We followed my mom inside and up some stairs to an office. To our surprise and confusion, it was our social worker's office. Those next moments were just a blur. All I remember is my mom and the social worker explaining that my mom couldn't take care of the three of us all together. It was too much for her, so she was going to keep my older sister, Roxanne, and my younger brother would stay with me in foster care. Ryan and I were left in that office with our social worker. I just remember screaming, crying, and trying to run after my mom and sister. I was being held back and felt helpless, defeated, and abandoned. These moments that I remember are not positive. They are sad and traumatic. They are moments I don't wish for anyone to experience. I look back not as a victim, but as a compassionate soul that sees a little child in those tough moments; my inner child that learned about compassion and empathy. I learned the values that I hold dear inside me today and I want to instill them in my daughter. This also taught me how important it is to make sure my daughter never feels abandoned and that she knows every single day how loved she is.

I'm grateful for my lessons and experiences, no matter how hard they were because I would not be who I am today if I hadn't gone through all the challenges I faced. Lessons are blessings. I now love who I am, and love who I'm growing into more and more every day. I love my strength and my resiliency. I love my heart, my soul, and my faith. I'm so incredibly grateful for Helen, who came into my life at the exact moment I needed her and taught me about God; she's truly an angel on earth.

I'm not trying to convince others that God is real or force my beliefs on anyone else. Whatever you believe is 100% okay. Your belief is a part of you; it is for your own soul's mission and journey here in this life. For you, God may be Allah, the Universe, energy, or a higher power. Or maybe you don't believe in any of the above, and that's fine. I'm only here to explain what my faith has done for me. My faith has given me the strength to love myself.

Years ago, I went through a series of self-development courses, spiritual development, and mindset practices. I was going to a women's healing circle every Wednesday evening and spiritual development every Sunday afternoon. On the days in between, I would go for nature walks, work out, and meet with my sister and two girlfriends who were also attending these things with me. I prayed and meditated every morning and night. I listened to positive and motivational audio recordings whenever I had the chance. I wasn't watching TV, though when I had time, I would read books like, *You Can Heal Your Life* by Louise Hay, *Wishes Fulfilled* by Wayne Dyer, *How to Hear Your Angels* by Doreen Virtue and *Think Like a Monk* by Jay Shetty.

I felt happy and was healing every day. I was feeling more and more confident, happy, and loving. I had great relationships. I felt the best in my mind, body, and soul than I ever had. I thought I was healed. I thought I had figured it out. I loved myself!

Certain things changed when the teacher I had become so connected with had to abruptly put the classes on hold. She was going through something personal and we never received any warnings; the classes just stopped. We were a group of positive and happy people, so we still met up and meditated. We committed ourselves to help each other stay on this amazing positive journey together. But then life happens and challenges can occur throughout some of our most positive moments! During this time, I was still dealing with a lot of emotional and verbal abuse from an ex-boyfriend. I was struggling as a single mom financially, emotionally, and mentally. I was in another relationship with someone I had thought was going to be my future, but that came crashing down and I felt completely blindsided. I was still working on my mindset, meditating, reading books, working out, and going to church while going through all of this, but I was also feeling moments of depression and anxiety.

A couple of years later, I lost my younger brother. This was one of the most terrible moments in my life. Nothing made sense. I was in shock and experienced terrible pain, anger, disbelief, and so many different emotions that I still can't even explain. During that time, I still had my faith, despite the sadness and everything else I was experiencing. I felt I understood life ending in a different way than I would have before because of all those spiritual teachings I had. It didn't make it easier; I still had to feel all the emotions, but it gave me a sense of understanding and knowing that my brother is always with me. I also remembered that everything is temporary. Not the loss; the loss is real and my life would never be the same, but the extreme pain and sadness that we call grief—that is always changing.

Another example of how grief affected my life occurred a couple of years ago when a grief hurricane came crashing into our lives after my stepmom was taken to the hospital. I call her my step mom but she was the last foster mom I had lived with. I lived with her from when I was 12-16 years old. We had kept in touch and she had become family. My daughter, Kayla, knew her as grandma. She had been struggling with many health issues over the years. Since this was during the Covid-19 pandemic, we weren't allowed to see her when she was taken to the hospital until they said her organs were failing. We each got to visit and say our goodbyes, and the next day she passed away. A couple of days after that, my ex-father-in-law (Kayla's grandpa from her dad's side) was diagnosed with cancer and was told he had two months to live. Kayla had just lost her grandma and now was losing her grandpa. Over the next couple of months, Kayla spent time with her grandpa, her dad, and the rest of her family as much as she could, all while keeping up a somewhat normal routine and also beginning the grieving process. Later, almost a month and a half after her grandpa passed, Kayla's dad unexpectedly suffered a heart attack. This was the cherry on top… in just three and a half months, my 13-year-old daughter lost her grandma, grandpa, and her dad. I call it a grief hurricane because there was so much grief all at once from every angle just swirling around, toppling over, and suffocating everyone. A lot of people lost these loved ones; everyone had their own unique, yet somewhat similar, ways of grieving. Although I was suffering from loss and grief as well, I thought about my daughter's pain first, since as a mom, we tend to put our children above ourselves. I couldn't bear the pain she was going through and I didn't know how to help her. She felt suffocated by me at times, but all I knew was to love her and be there through it all.

Loss is a funny thing because it's never just the person we lose; it's their presence, their touch, and their energy; it's the future, the safety, and the promises. Their physical life is over but it still feels so unfinished to the loved ones left behind. A deep loss is always a pivotal moment in life. It changes our lives permanently and sometimes this also includes people that you thought would always be close to you. Through all those losses, we grew closer together with some people and farther apart from others. I experienced losing some family and friends due to physical losses, which I realize now is part of life. Sometimes loss shows you the truth. At the time, it was tough but I do know that I am close to the people who my values align with, and not everyone is meant to walk through your whole life with you. This is where self-love and acceptance come in. If you expect people to do what you would do in a situation, then you will be disappointed. You need to choose to either forgive and accept them for who they are, or forgive and walk away. Some people are only meant to be in your life for a small period of time, while others may be in your life for longer. Everyone is meant to teach you something. Acceptance and awareness of that are key.

As Oprah said, "Forgiveness is giving up the hope that the past could have been any different; it's accepting the past for what it was, and using this moment and this time to help yourself move forward."

And moving forward is exactly what my family and I have done. In this last year and a half, we have seen some big changes. I moved with my boyfriend and my daughter to Kelowna, British Columbia. This was a tough transition because although I moved homes a lot as a child, I have only ever lived in the Edmonton area until moving to Kelowna. It was a beautiful transition in so many ways, as well including the connection to nature and the beautiful views. I also have noticed such beautiful and pure energy when it comes to so many of the amazing people I have met here, particularly the women in business I meet when I attend many networking events. This is a place where many people have moved from somewhere else in the world, so everyone is looking to connect and it's so nice to feel the support and love. I still hold my family and friends from Edmonton very close; I do go back often and they also come to visit. I try to convince them all to move… maybe one day!

Moving to Kelowna has definitely been an adjustment, but the growth my family and I have experienced has been incredible. My relationship with my boyfriend, Gabriel, has evolved in more ways than I could express. He has been such an amazing support, not only through many hard times in my life but also throughout my daughter's journey of losing her father. He has never tried to replace her dad and has given us space when we needed it and support when it was needed. He always makes sure to bring up positive memories of her dad in conversations with her. He truly has been a blessing in both of our lives. My daughter going through such loss at the age of 13, then us deciding to move provinces just over a year later, was such a tough time as she was in the middle of semesters in Grade 10 when we made the move. I was worried that she would push back, but I explained to her right from the beginning to please keep an open mind, that we can visit often, that family and friends can come to visit us, and that if it doesn't work out, we could always move back. To my surprise, she was a lot more open than I expected, and even though she missed a lot of people, she has grown, developed, and also healed so much since we moved. I do not doubt that we are where we need to be.

Lessons I've Learned and Mindset Tips

Self-love is self-awareness. It's being aware of what you love about yourself, what your faith means to you, and knowing that your beliefs and faith are right for who you are.

I'm not saying you can't learn about other people's faith, or that your beliefs can't change and grow. We are always evolving, growing, and changing in who we are, so it's a natural thing that our beliefs may change or evolve over different periods and experiences in our lives.

It's important to recognize that you are a special unique soul, and there is not one person exactly like you in this huge growing Universe. I believe God made us this way. I believe that once you really let that sink in, you will understand that you were born into this life for a reason and a purpose. You have your own special and individual gift to share with this world. If you didn't, why would you be so unique? If we didn't all have a reason to be here and something to give this life, then we would all be the same, wouldn't we? If this life was just a series of similar events and people being born to serve their time on this earth, it would look more like a bunch of robots doing work in a production plant. Seems silly, right? We are all different—I like to think of us as snowflakes; every one of us is so completely individual and beautiful all at the same time! We all have a special makeup, a different and completely unique DNA. You are here in this life for a reason. You are special and you are meant to share your gifts with this world.

It can be as simple as being kind to everyone you meet. Smiling at strangers because you don't realize how that one smile might just make their entire day. Being grateful to everyone around you for whatever it is they have to share. Understanding that money isn't everything, and money does not make you a good person or a bad person. Material things don't make you who you are, nor do they define you. Your character is a reflection of your soul and who you are inside is your gift. Share it with everyone, every single day.

Self-love is self-commitment. It is following through on your commitments to yourself. It is waking up when the alarm clock goes off because that's the time you set it for. You made that commitment to yourself the day before so you should follow through. It is self-care, committing to self-care, and doing the things that you know you need to do—taking time and space for yourself, and your mental health. Self-love is a lot of things; it's not perfect and it's not being perfect. You will never be perfect. Everybody who is born is here for a reason; for lessons to learn and to grow. You can feel like you're the most connected person by going through mindset training every single day, meditating, and living in the present moment. You could be a monk and live the simplest life through love, though you still won't be perfect. You will still be learning every day. You have to accept yourself. Self-acceptance is self-love. Accepting yourself for who you are truly, imperfectly, and unapologetically.

Another important lesson to me is about having strength. I'm so grateful for my strength. God must think I'm a very strong person to have given me so many lessons throughout my life. One mantra that I have said over and over when dealing with some really tough stuff is, "If God brings you to it, He will bring you through it."

I used to feel ashamed of where I came from; being in foster care and feeling unwanted and abandoned. I remember when telling a friend in school that I was in a foster home, and I would always say, "Please don't tell anyone," as though it was a big secret that made me a bad person. I now feel blessed, grateful, and proud. I accept who I am. I am strong, I am resilient, and I am amazing! I accept what I've experienced and all of my lessons because they allow me to help others through similar experiences and that is a true gift from God.

Forgiveness and letting go of what is not serving you is self-love. As unique as we all are, so are our values and our perceptions, which lead to our choices. We are all living in this world but experiencing our lessons in very different ways. There are things that we can relate to, but sometimes it's not easy to understand where someone is coming from or what they are going through. Loss is an example of how many different people can experience the loss of one person in so many different ways.

Remember…

Treat yourself like someone you love. Say this to yourself every day: "I am enough. I am loved. I am imperfectly perfectly me. I love myself."

Loving yourself means doing what you feel is right for you and your family. It is not allowing fear of change to hold you back because once you make that jump, it may just be the best thing you have ever done! I have learned to be brave, and more confident, and to make a decision and do it! I continue to learn there are so many amazing and beautiful souls, and we all want one main thing: to receive and give love. I believe that love is the most important thing in this entire Universe, and if everything was pure love there would not be any room for fear, jealousy, anger, etc. Love overpowers all. It is so pure and it is the only thing that truly conquers that negative self-talk that we all have experienced. You know the little voice inside our heads that tell us we aren't enough? Or that we can't do something? If you take one thing from me today, I hope it's to please be aware of this little voice, and any time you hear it, counteract it with a positive thought, such as, *I love myself, I am worthy, I can do anything, or I am a beautiful soul and I have a unique gift to share with the world.*

I believe love is the soul of the world, which is why I want to leave you with a scripture from the bible that I have as a tattoo, and I believe these are such powerful words that are so true. Live by these words and watch your life change in the most incredible ways:

"Let all that you do, be done in Love"

Corinthians 16:14

Lessons Learned:

1. I've learned that my lessons are a gift. They have formed me into who I am today. As long as I'm still physically here I will continue to learn and grow every day!
2. I've learned that my character and integrity are so important & doing the right thing no matter who is watching is being true to myself. I learned to always to live by my values but also to have self-compassion as we are all human.
3. I've learned that once I make a decision just do it- I am unstoppable!

Mindset Tips:

1. Be aware of the negative self talk. Anytime something negative comes into your mind replace with with a positive & loving thought/affirmation. Visualize what you want and feel the emotions behind it- This is so powerful!
2. Be grateful for all of your experiences positive or negative because they will all teach you something- write down your gratitude daily. As you start writing you will feel that shift..
3. You are amazing- Know your worth. Be open to other perceptions/beliefs but don't discount your own faith. You are here to share your gift and love with this world. Believe that and show yourself love, kindness and compassion every day!

Aha Moments and Self-Reflections

Note your Thoughts

Sarah Ommen

Sarah Ommen's mission in life is to show people what they are capable of if they start listening to their own inner knowing and stop listening to the "should" that has been placed on them by the outer world. She wears many hats as she traverses through the world; she is a healer, a witnesser, a giving soul, a transmuter of energy, and above all else, a lover. Sarah has an amazing family who has moved through the land of ups and downs but has come out greater on the other side. In her life on Earth, Sarah has become a wife, mother, speech-language pathologist, healer, photographer, certified life coach with a focus on the teen years, a dancer, and now a published author, among many other things. Having ADHD and a passion for passion will do that to you.

Sarah has become a master of her own energy by doing the work. Although she is now in a good place, that was not always the case. She was diagnosed with depression and anxiety at a young age and has had to fight her way through it for many years. This fight is what has propelled her to help others to become their own best advocate and highest guru. She knows you don't need someone to tell you what to do, but someone to show you how to help yourself. That is where true peace and self-love can be found.

Sarah would like to thank her cheerleaders and inspirations: her husband, mother, children, nana, the queens at JNL coaching, the instructors and other students at Seacoast Stilettos and many friends who inspire her daily. She knows that your tribe really impacts your whole vibe!

Connect with Sarah:

www.sarahommen.com
https://www.instagram.com/sarahommen_theinspiredteen
https://www.facebook.com/groups/292876804742337/

Chapter 15

How I Loved Myself Healthy

By Sarah Ommen

Who is she and why does she look dead inside? Her eyes used to sparkle and now they look flat. This is what I thought about myself on New Year's Eve of 2015 when I looked at a photo of myself at the table as we celebrated with friends to ring in the new year. That was it. I was done being unhappy in my own skin. It was time for change.

What does it mean to be "unhappy in my skin?" For the longest time, I couldn't tell you, but I knew it was a feeling of loathing and pain that could not be pinpointed. There was no specific thing that could be identified that left me unhappy and longing for more. I had the ideal life: The education, the career, the husband, the house, the two kids (a boy and a girl), yet I felt empty and unhappy. I can only describe the empty I felt as a feeling of numbness. Believing that you should feel joy from getting exactly what you want but feeling shame because it just wasn't there. Then I would judge myself for feeling unfulfilled, empty, and unhappy when so many people would love to have the life I lived. It was a vicious cycle of self-loathing, pain, and shame for not being grateful for what I had. It left me wondering if this was just what life was; a never-ending cycle of simply surviving, one moment to the next, and hoping for little glimpses of joy from time to time. I was surviving, but far from thriving. I was not enjoying the life I had worked so hard to build, and the guilt I felt because of it was eating me up.

This loathing was invisible to everyone on the outside. It manifested in weight gain, a few more drinks than normal, a lack of boundaries, continuous people pleasing, and overspending to numb the pain. Just a few of the things that our culture views as "normal." Nothing that sticks out and says you need help.

How did I get here? Let us take this all back a bit.... I made my life plan when I was 15 years old. My good girl persona was imperative at that time to save face with my family and community. Being a child of a young mother and having a father who had made some poor choices, I dealt with a lot of talk. People are so judgmental, and it was my duty to show them! I laid my plan and began the challenging work at making it come true. Undergrad, masters, married, house, babies, and all by the time I was 30. I mean, that is the American dream, right? To have it all. Let's throw in the white picket fence for good measure (ours was white plastic but same difference). I had to be as perfect as humanly possible. My ego's life depended on it.

I made it all come true. No veering, no stopping, just sheer drive and determination. I achieved my masters at 26, met my husband the same year, got engaged at 27, married at 28, we had our son at 29, and our daughter just before we turned 31. There it was! My dream life manifested. Yet, why was I so empty and struggling to enjoy this life I built? Do not get me wrong; I love my husband and my children. I loved the life we were living, but I felt like something was missing.

We were living in California at this time, and we made the decision to move back to New Hampshire. I knew this was going to solve all the problems in my life. I just knew it. Being near family and old friends would help, right? When (insert desire) happens, THEN I will be happy. Do you ever say this to yourself? I feel like as a society we are constantly saying I will be happy when... insert goal or dream here.

Guess what? All the "when" happened and I still felt empty. Every relationship I had suffered. I had put expectations on my husband to make me happy. He should just know what I need. If he loved me enough, he would read my mind. My children were my pride and joy, the people I knew I wanted in my life since my first memories, yet I found myself short with them and not being the best mom that I could be. My friendships were centered around drinking, spending money, gossiping, and complaining.

I had no idea that I was, in fact, the problem. I had no capability to see my positive attributes and support my own victories. I was constantly striving to be better, do better, and never appreciating what I had achieved in life, and it was backfiring in the worst way. I was never enough. What I did was never enough. But why? Because I had never been taught to love myself. I had never been exposed to emotional intelligence. I had no idea how to handle my emotions and myself. I just knew how to keep striving for more and put on a show for everyone else. There was no self-love, self-care, gratitude, or grace for me. I was as close to a robot as a human can be. I was programmed by society to be this ever-perfect female and not show signs of imperfection or weakness. I would dissociate regularly and just go through the motions of my daily life.

When I showed emotion, I was a drama queen or a head case, probably because I lacked the knowledge that emotions are important to feel. But when they consume and dictate you, that is where the problem lies. I would fall hard and fast into an emotional abyss because it was all or nothing in my head. I was either dissociated or riding the hot-mess-express of emotions. Plus, through the process of how the universe works (like attracts like), the people I attracted into my life shared my same lack of emotional intelligence. How could we all understand each other when we had no basic understanding of ourselves?

That New Year's Eve picture was the spark that ignited an inferno! I decided that I'd had enough and was ready for change. My journey to self-love started as a weight-loss journey. If I were just skinny, I would certainly be happy. If this happens, then I will feel…. (Insert desired emotional state). You know the drill! We talked about it already. Why do we need validation of our worth? Why can't we recognize that we are innately and divinely worthy just by existing? Another tangent as I look back at the old me and feel so sad and sorry for her, but also grateful for her strength.

The journey to self-love is not always radical; sometimes it must be slow and methodical. Sometimes you do not even realize you are on it because it is masquerading as something else altogether. Perhaps it is a weight-loss journey, a new career or degree, or a new project or hobby. You just know something is missing. Usually that something is you knowing your own worth, and that you are worthy of love from the most important person in your life—yourself—but I digress. It is a lesson that takes time to learn.

If you can resonate with my story, then let me take you on an adventure—the adventure of loving myself healthy. You see, for most of my life, I tried to shame myself into being "healthy" (aka skinny), never believing I was good enough, strong enough, skinny enough, or smart enough. I could always be better. While you can always improve, the real flex is loving yourself exactly as you are in this moment, imperfections and all.

What started with a picture that made me sad, mad, and motivated, became my personal mission to stop breaking promises to myself. I was going to set small goals and hit them to build up my wellness stamina. The first goal was to lose weight (because it is almost always the first goal when you are unhappy). At 38 years old, that was not as easy as it used to be and in the first two months, I only lost between 3-5 pounds. It would have been so easy to give up, but I kept searching for something that would work for me instead. The next thing I did was make the decision to start flossing my teeth every single day instead of doing it randomly. It was something small, but it was a promise that I could keep to help build my consistency muscle. My major promise to myself was that I was not going to give up and give in this time. I knew it would not be linear, but I also knew that it would be worth it. Whatever I found had to be better than how I was living.

So much changed when I decided to change, and truly decided that change was not optional but imperative. I was taking my health into my own hands and people were noticing. I was attracting like-minded people into my life. I was reading more books about self-development. I was going for hikes with my family, which fed all of our souls, and dates with my husband where we reconnected after years of unintentional disconnection on my part. I was taking the initiative to MAKE my own JOY. I was not relying on someone or something else to provide it for me. This was new, scary, and liberating! I was caring for myself in ways I had no idea I needed. I was showing my children what a happy mom can look like and how they can also live a happy life by choice. They definitely noticed the change in me when they were younger and now that they are teens, they comment on how I am too positive for them sometimes! I'm grateful they don't really remember a lot about the old me. I'm not proud of who I was in survival mode.

I started working out again. I had lost the drive and passion when the kids were toddlers and life just got so "busy" that it was just not a priority anymore. I bribed myself to lift weights again with this amazing lemon passion crunch protein bar that I found. It was my reward for getting to the gym and I would only eat it if I lifted. You must find those little things that work for you to get you motivated and moving. After a while, I reconnected with my love of working out and the dopamine hit that resulted. It takes time to get there, though. When you first start or restart, it can be a daunting experience until you get to that other side where it is required for your well-being. Just remember that motivation is fleeting; you must build up your consistency and dedication to yourself. Relying on motivation will get you nowhere fast.

My body was well on its way to being the healthiest that I could be by the time I hit 40. Forty is a big milestone for a woman and I was happy to have this goal to get me there. The problem with change is it scares people. They would talk behind my back about how I had "changed," like it was a terrible thing. The only thing we can guarantee in life is that change is inevitable and it's up to you to decide which direction you want it to go in. My change was lighting up the darkness in people and it was triggering them to react. People who believe they are incapable or unworthy of change view your change as a direct attack. I recently saw the statement that when you grow your light and start shining bright, you must also regulate your nervous system to take the hits from the people living in the dark. This was something that I was not prepared for.

The words of others started to break me down and get into my head. I almost gave up on everything I was working on. I wanted to go back to the old me because it was easier, and people liked her better. Cue people-pleaser Sarah. I had no idea that if everyone liked you, chances are you did not like yourself. Here is where it all changed; I dove deep and hard into learning everything there was to know about mindset, self-development, and self-love. I wish I could pinpoint what it was, but something triggered the idea in my mind that it was IN MY HEAD and that was what needed to be worked on and addressed. My brain was holding me back the whole time. I read at least 50-something self-help and development books and then I got to work on implementing what I liked and could take with me.

I took a course in neurolinguistic programming (NLP) because the brain fascinates me. I also minored in psychology and have always loved to learn about the inner-workings of the mind. In that class, I learned that I am a series of programs that have been written through life, upbringing, community, culture, safety, etc. I started looking at what programs needed to be rewritten or deleted. I started questioning every move I made and asking if this was me or my programming. Where had I picked this up and why? Did it feel like me or was it something I did because it was what I was told to do? I began to question my beliefs, thoughts, and feelings. I learned so much about myself during this time, and I continue to use this method when I find myself strongly reacting to something. Is this about me or does it upset my programming? This class was so powerful that I took it in 2017 and have not had an almond joy since because of the rewriting that was done in minutes. It also meant my brain was ready for change!

NLP was a great jumping off place; however, the real work was applying all that I had learned. Gratitude was another key concept that I learned. To sit in gratitude for all that you have leaves you open to more blessings from the universe. It is not bragging or boasting, and it puts you into the vibration to attract more of what you desire. It is not woo-woo and is something everyone can benefit from immediately. Gratitude can change your mindset in moments. When you appreciate what you have in your life, your brain chemistry starts to change. Try it now by naming one person you are grateful for, one food you are grateful for, one sound you are grateful for, and one smell you are grateful for. My favorite activity to do with my students and clients is to tell them to list everything they can think of knowing that tomorrow they will only wake up with the things they were grateful for today. People can dig deeper with this activity, and it makes them open to all that they have instead of all that they lack. Lack mentality is a hindrance to so many. Our lives are not scarce or lacking. They are vivid, abundant, and beautiful, but if your mind cannot see what is in front of it, then it is hard to believe these truths. Your mind believes what you tell it, so you must focus on what you want out of life. Do you want a happy, healthy, joyful, and abundant life full of love? Of course, you do! And believing you deserve it is the first step.

Another key concept to my success and breakthroughs was learning that I cannot pour from an empty cup. Self-care is imperative to keep my cup overflowing so that I can give freely to others without depleting myself. There is the traditional self-care that includes pampering and caring for your outside appearance and, while I do all of that too, my inner self-care is where my abundance comes from. I care for my body by providing it with nourishing food, water, and supplements because it is my temple and the only one that I have. I move my body every day in some meaningful way that always includes stretching and inversions, plus either cardiovascular activity or weights. Lifting weights is so important for women as we age; I wish more people knew the value of it beyond the aesthetics. I mean, I love looking good, but these workouts are self-care for my body and my mind. My overall health depends on not just me not finding the motivation for these workouts, but also building the consistency to do them. You do not rely on motivation to shower or brush your teeth; you just know it needs to be done and the same goes for your workouts. My advice to you is to set aside 5-10 minutes and just start moving, stretching, lifting light weights, dancing or taking a walk. I hear women tell me they do not have time, but you make time for what is important to you. Try changing "I don't have time" to "it's not a priority to me" and see how that feels in your mind.

My favorite thing I have developed over the years is my morning routine. It varies in length but there is always time for my mantra and my gratitude. As soon as my brain stirs and my eyes open, I say my mantra:

I am happy.

I am healthy.

I am grateful.

I am loved.

And I am living in abundance.

I repeat it as often as I need while I do my morning ritual. Next, I make my bed. Everyday! It is one of those consistency building rituals that help you feel successful early in the day. Of course, I brush my teeth and wash the sleepiness out of my eyes next. Then, it is to the kitchen for my adaptogens and marine collagen. Next comes my favorite part, which is my moving meditation. Having spondylarthritis means my body does not love to move in the morning, so I move gently and methodically to give it a chance to catch up. I take to my quiet office with my Hz meditation music and pick which frequency I am feeling for the day. Do I need to send love out before me when I know there will be a difficult day? Do I need healing due to pain? Do I want to bring forth more positivity? There is a frequency for all of it. I also pick my crystal of the moment and add it into my practice. I then begin with stretches as I clear my mind and bring forth what I desire to feel in my body. I have an amazing inversion chair that I use in the process for stretching and inversions. I spend about 5-10 minutes on this moving meditation, and it is worth waking up 10-15 minutes earlier to set my day off in this beautiful way. The last step in the morning routine is coffee. I love my coffee and my new favorite is a mushroom blend for immunity or brain health. I do not even look at my phone until all of this is complete. In fact, my phone has slept in my kitchen every night since COVID-19 started and I was finding myself waking up to read all the scary information in the middle of the night. It was no way to live. Besides, letting hundreds of people into your bedroom is never a good thing.

Another wellness hack that I have implemented is to rid my life of toxins. We cannot avoid environmental toxins. I am not a hardcore person when it comes to this but I take simple steps. I switched to natural cleaning products, I began a weekly toxin cleanse (a 24-36 hour supported fast), I limited access to the news or other fear-mongering platforms, and I cleaned up my social media and "hid" certain people so that their views were not imposed on me without my consent. The toxins we are exposed to are not always physical, so be sure to take stock of the emotional and spiritual toxins all around you and change what you can.

To recap, small daily action steps can change your life tremendously. Start by adding in the things I mentioned that you find easiest. Can you do a daily gratitude check? Can you make a healthy dinner? Can you change some of your cleaning products? Do you have five minutes to meditate instead of watching Netflix or scrolling on Instagram? I achieved major change by taking small actions daily. I believe you can too, and I want to hear all about it!

Four lessons I've learned that I want to share with you:

- You will make time for what you view as important, and if you don't view yourself as important then that needs to change right now. You are your only constant in your life. Everything else can and will change.

- You are worthy of reaching for all those dreams that your head keeps telling you that you will not achieve or do not deserve.
- The negative self-talk in your head is not you! It is a result of conditioning from a society that wants to keep women down. Most of our society does not realize their thoughts are from conditioning and not their true authentic self. Always ask if this is truly you or something someone else taught or put on you.
- Trying new things is important to your growth. You cannot learn by doing what you are already good at. I started dance lessons at 44 years young and I was scared out of my mind but I kept going. Now my dance classes are a big source of joy and growth in my life. Do the thing and do it scared! Ask your inner child what she wants and go do it!

Three Mindset Tips I feel everyone should know:

- Speak to yourself as if you were talking to your 10-year-old self. Would you say the same unkind and untrue words to her?
- Create a morning routine, be it intricate or small, to get your mind set up intentionally for the entire brut-iful day ahead of you (brut-iful implies that you will take the "good" with the "bad" and realize they are all part of the human experience).
- Be conscious of your phone, social media and news intake, and do not let it into your bedroom or your mind before you have set your intentions for the day.

The overall message I want to leave you with here is that you have the power inside of you to become who you want to be. You are powerful beyond measure and when I finally realized that I had this power, my entire life changed and so can yours! Small, daily, consistent actions will add up because the compound effect is real. You may not see the change but keep taking the steps and you will get closer to where you want to be. While you are taking these beautiful and, at times, hard steps, remember to love yourself along the way. Celebrate where you are, who you are, and all you have done to make it this far. Life can be hard, but it is also beautiful. We are worthy of all the love, joy, and abundance that the universe has to offer. It is ours for the taking so go out and take it Goddesses!

Lessons Learned:

1. You are worthy of reaching for all those dreams.
2. Trying new things is important to your growth.
3. You are your only constant in your life. Everything else can and will change.

Mindset Tips:

1. Speak to yourself as if you were talking to your 10-year-old self.
2. Be conscious of your phone, social media, and news intake; do not let it into your bedroom or your mind before you have set your intentions for the day.
3. You have the power inside of you to become who you want to be. You are powerful beyond measure.

Aha Moments and Self-Reflections

Note your Thoughts

Shannan Stella Roberts

Shannan Stella Roberts is a mother, multi-preneur, and nature lover with a friendly adventurous spirit. She lives an intrepid life, makes friends everywhere she goes, and continually challenges herself to learn and experience new things. Throughout her professional career, Shannan has advocated for diversity and inclusion, cultural awareness, and socio-economic initiatives. She is co-owner of Prep Academy Tutors of Interior British Columbia, which seeks to be the gold standard in private in-home and virtual tutoring and educational services. Shannan believes that every student learns differently and loves serving families so that parents can trust their child is receiving the individual instruction they need. She works as a business and export advisor and leads collaborative partnerships between industry and Indigenous businesses and communities.

Shannan brings a passion for people, community, and business to all of her work. She is the Vice President of Kelowna Women in Business and an active member of her community. She loves and strives to be of service by helping clients identify and achieve their goals. She undertakes this by sharing her knowledge and lived experience through teaching, advising, coaching, mentoring, and most of all, facilitating connections. Shannan's own goals of becoming an author and public speaker are already unfolding in 2023.

Shannan strives to embody her gifts of being an Activator, Includer, and Maximizer, and sharing her positivity. She is co-founder of Northern Youth Leadership, which provides personal growth, leadership opportunities, and connections that empower young people to create positive change. For Shannan, self-love is knowing her strengths and trusting herself. She is empowered to create her reality, knows what she wants, and chooses it daily.

Connect with Shannan:
https://www.linkedin.com/in/sschimmelmann
https://www.facebook.com/shannan.schimmelmann
https://www.instagram.com/inspiredactionacademy/

Chapter 16

Knowing Who I am and Choosing it Daily

By Shannan Stella Roberts

My journey of self-love has everything to do with self-awareness, and clarity about my values, strengths, and dreams. I have learned to trust myself and take responsibility for the life I am creating. Last year, I felt like my life was falling apart. Something inside of me was calling me to remember who I am and my soul's purpose. My intention in writing this chapter is to share my journey to self, through loss and challenging times. For me, leaning into my strengths was my catalyst to embrace self-love. I hope the lessons I've learned resonate and inspire you to celebrate your unique strengths and live your best life.

My story begins in Timmins, Ontario, where I enjoyed a simple childhood in a loving home. From a young age, my parents encouraged me to live a happy life, to dream big, and to nurture self-development. My mom and dad are both hard-working, community-minded, and extremely supportive. I am the eldest of four biological siblings (Lance, Tamarah, and Tiffinnea), and two bonus brothers (Keith and Douglas), whom our family fostered since they were 3 and 5 years old. From the age of 3 until 10, I attended Catholic Francophone elementary schools and otherwise spent most of my free time in nature at my grandparents' farm; swimming in the lake and playing in the forest surrounding our home. I was a friendly and curious girl, always up for trying anything new: from skating and snowmobiling, tap and jazz dancing, to baseball and community talent shows. I come from a large family and feel so blessed to have had the gift of spending my childhood with grandparents, great-grandparents, and many aunts, uncles, and cousins. My mom was a stay-at-home parent and also worked in the "gig economy" as a college instructor, professional cake decorator, seamstress, crafter, and later as a daycare provider. My dad worked in the mining industry, which led to a career opportunity and our family moved to Yellowknife, Northwest Territories—the land of the midnight sun and diamond capital of North America. Growing up, money was tight, but we always had everything we needed. It didn't occur to me until grade four or five that some people judged others based on financial status. As a teen, I recall feeling underprivileged because we couldn't afford to buy popular brands and trending fashions, and I wasn't able to participate in the same opportunities as some of my friends. Certain hobbies, sports, private school, and travel experiences were not in the budget for my family. Memories of feeling poor make me feel guilty and ashamed of myself, especially when I consider true poverty and famine in Canada and many parts of the world. It has also impacted my attitude and persistence toward achieving my goal of financial freedom.

When our family moved to the Northwest Territories at the end of the summer of 1988, Yellowknife felt like a bold new world as a young girl from Northern Ontario. I started my first day of grade six the week we arrived. Making friends at school ended up being a lot of fun. Throughout my school years, I was very involved, and incredibly curious to meet anyone that spoke another language, lived in a foreign country, or practiced a different culture, religion, or belief system. In grade 12, my passion to learn more about culture, languages, and the world at large inspired me to become an American Field Service (AFS) exchange student in Brazil for a full year. I have always been an avid reader, and especially love biographies and personal development books. It was during this year abroad that I read the *Celestine Prophecy*, which focuses on a search for a sacred manuscript in a Peruvian rainforest. The book encouraged me to contemplate the meaning of enlightenment and to be open to new ways of thinking, growing, expanding, and helping others to do the same. My year away from home made me feel courageous and independent. The experience was transformational in so many ways and influenced my personal development and how I relate to the world at large.

Upon my return to Canada, I dove into my continued education and career in hospitality. I registered in the Hotel & Restaurant Management Diploma program from the School of Business at Camosun College in Victoria, British Columbia. Student life in Victoria was exhilarating and liberating in so many ways. I enjoyed every course in my program, and the challenge to learn and grow. I was meeting like-minded people and creating lifelong friendships. I chose to participate in the Cooperative Education Program, as I loved the practicality of work experience for academic credit. This opportunity led to my first work term living in the Rocky Mountains in Canmore, Alberta. I focused on my full-time job as Catering Coordinator and launched a new party planning and event management side hustle. The culture in the mountains was a beautiful blend of relaxation with a passion for outdoor recreation. It inspired me to spend as much time as possible in nature. Being in nature made me feel more connected to myself, and gave me time to be still and reflect. While living in Canmore, I negotiated my second cooperative education work term to be an international work placement based in Seattle, USA through the Radisson brand of hotels. This was such an exciting role, delivering the guest services program called "Making It Right!" across the Americas. I would be able to travel for work and use my language skills. At this time in my life, I spoke English, French, and Portuguese (Brazilian), and was learning Spanish and German in college. As it happens, this would not be my adventure to live and story to tell. While living in Canmore working at the Radisson Hotel chain in 1999, I began experiencing very serious health challenges. I was run down and unable to recognize the stress I was placing on myself. I was diagnosed with an auto-immune disorder that led to my return home to Yellowknife, where I needed my family to support my recovery to better health.

Moving back to Yellowknife, after graduating from college in 2000, shattered my dream to live and work internationally. Over the next year, I had to concentrate on becoming healthy again. I continued to work in hospitality and decided to complete my Bachelor of Business Administration virtually at Athabasca University. In 2001, I knew it was time for a new challenge, and I secured a job in finance and economic development for a developmental agency called the NWT Business Development and Investment Corporation. During this time, I discovered my passion for long-distance running and marathons. Jogging outdoors and on trails became a way for me to clear my head, reduce stress, and keep my mind and body strong and fit.

While completing my studies and working full-time, I met a special person named RJ through common friends at a Halloween party. For several years I had dated casually, but I didn't have any long-term relationship experience. RJ and I had a magnetic attraction and I spent nearly all of my free time with him. He was a commuter and worked at a remote diamond mine on a two-week rotation between home and work. After about five months of dating, we moved in together.

At this time, I kept very busy with work and school and didn't spend very much time with my family or friends. Some of my siblings were living in other Canadian provinces as we were all trying to find our way as young adults. My two youngest brothers, eight and six years younger than me, were living in Yellowknife, and we would visit occasionally to play a board game, enjoy a movie night, or have a meal together. Keith and Douglas are biological brothers born in Kugaaruk (Pelly Bay),

Nunavut. Growing up, I felt a very strong connection to both of them. After high school graduation, Keith started working at a diamond mine, bought himself a car, and was saving for his education. He was a gentle and kind person, very handsome, athletic, intelligent, and hard-working. Keith had many friends and seemed to be on a good path. Little did I know, he was struggling with depression and turned to drugs. One evening, I received an emergency call from the hospital to say Keith had overdosed and there was a chance he may not survive and could suffer severe brain damage. I was the only family member in Yellowknife at that time. Seeing my little brother in the Intensive Care Unit on the hospital bed, attached to so many machines, cords, and pumps, and not knowing if he would survive, was terrifying. I remember feeling flooded with intense emotion; my breathing was shallow, I couldn't think clearly, and nothing going on around me seemed to matter. I felt so afraid, completely helpless, and at the mercy of the medical team who were doing everything possible to save his life. Amid this crisis, my lone thought was centered on Keith's survival. It was impossible to relax, prepare and eat proper meals, or sleep. It was non-stop worry, waiting at the hospital and by the phone for updates. I was grateful to have the support and comfort of my family and friends through this difficult time.

Over the next couple of months, Keith made a miraculous full physical recovery. Sadly, he didn't find a way to step out of his depression and continued to struggle for years, mostly in silence. Conversations about mental health were not yet commonplace. Resources and tools were underdeveloped and unknown to me. My life continued to be very focused on my career, and I began jogging more regularly, which was great for my mental health as a stress reliever, and an outlet to find mental clarity. In 2003, I met a colleague who inspired me to train for, and run, my first marathon. Long-distance running became so rewarding that I challenged myself to run a marathon every year. Marathon running is one of the ways I have chosen to experience the world. There are few things I love more than exploring a city or trail in a new country.

Throughout the challenges that I faced while supporting my brother Keith through his mental health struggles, working and studying full-time, my relationship with RJ was deepening. I had fallen in love with his free spirit, easygoing nature, and sense of adventure. We enjoyed a very active life and shared similar values. We dreamed about fun places in the world to travel and explore, we invested in real estate, we played sports, we went to concerts, and had so many fun experiences. Our relationship was passionate and full of optimism, with a focus on health and fitness, and trust. Since he was a commuter, the reality was that we had large chunks of time together and we spent a lot of time independently of one another. Together we were beginning to build the life of our dreams, and in August 2005, RJ proposed to me along the West Coast Trail. We were "Mauied" (married) on April 14, 2006. Soon after our honeymoon, we were thrilled to find out I was pregnant, and I was accepted to the Executive Management, Master in Business Administration (MBA) Program at Royal Roads University in Victoria. I became a mom in early 2007 to a beautiful healthy baby girl. While on maternity leave, I loved having my new infant at my side everywhere I went, even throughout my graduate student life.

At the same time, I was experiencing so much bliss and happiness in my world, my heart was also breaking into a million pieces. Unbeknownst to me, my youngest sibling, Douglas, was going through a dreadfully dark time in his life. Douglas was the baby of our family, the life of the party, wise, charismatic, generous, and a dreamer. Of all my siblings, he was the one that shared my love for board games the most. We spent hours playing chess, Scrabble, Monopoly, dice, and cards. He was 21 years old, employed, had many friends, and a girlfriend he loved very much. He hadn't yet decided which direction he wanted to focus his education and career. Comedy was his passion and a reoccurring theme for several years. I believe he would have been a huge success.

In the summer of 2008, while I was pregnant with my second daughter, I received news that Douglas had taken his life. I will never forget my feelings of shock, disbelief, and devastation. The news took my breath away, my whole body ached, and I bawled non-stop for days. I was confused and struggled to think of any happy thoughts. I remember not being able to open my eyes because they were so puffy, and not having the energy to roll out of bed. I can recall some sweet memories, including caring friends and colleagues that delivered me food, while I took time to grieve. To this day, I have intense memories of how these dishes tasted, and how they nourished my body.

Tragically, after surviving the loss of Douglas only five short months earlier, and still pregnant, my brother Keith chose the same fate and ended his life. It was the most shaken and traumatized I have ever been in my life. It felt like—and was—full-blown emotional overwhelm. In some ways, this experience felt vastly different. There was a part of my shattered heart that was gone, never to be hurt again. One big difference is that Keith left our family the most beautiful and heartfelt letter with his last wishes. His letter felt like an opportunity to honor him and understand the pain and suffering he was desperate to escape. My family and friends were compassionate and supportive as we healed together, but it took a long time. I was angry and felt abandoned by my brothers. I believed the agony of such deep sorrow would never end. I have since learned to accept my brothers' decision was theirs to make and not about me. I found a way to heal my heart through forgiveness and cherishing our good memories.

About a month later and a few days into 2009, we welcomed our second daughter to the world. I was halfway through my

MBA studies and absolutely loved student life. RJ and I decided to move from Yellowknife to Kelowna, B.C., to raise our family near relatives. We both liked the idea of hot sunny summers and mild winters. I loved everything about settling into my new town and, over the years, have built a wonderful community of friends through volunteering, entrepreneurship, and sport. I am proud of myself for becoming a volunteer running coach at the YMCA within weeks of relocating to Kelowna. I learned that friendships and connections built on healthy shared interests are one of the most delightful treasures in life.

The majority of my early years in Kelowna were focused on motherhood. I have loved every stage of life with both of my daughters from their infancy to their teenage years. It has been more magnificent than I could have imagined and is undeniably my most joyous and rewarding life experience.

At the beginning of 2020, before COVID-19 shut the world down, I thought my life was on track. I was married and a mom of two thriving daughters and two cats. I was comfortable in our family home and had a lovely garden in a friendly neighborhood. I had many friends and spent a lot of time in nature doing activities that bring me happiness. I had an incredible business partner that I relied on and believed in, and loved working from home as an entrepreneur. But, by springtime, the pandemic had turned into a disaster for my consulting business, which came to a screeching halt. My new start-up business faced so many Covid-related restrictions, hurdles, and delays to our wine and spirit industry travel and event services. It was one frustrating challenge after another, and repeated strategy changes. I built my identity as a financially successful business consultant and entrepreneur. My lack of employment income was causing anxiety and a loss of confidence in myself. I had fears of not being able to provide for my family and afford the lifestyle we were living. Financial success represents stability and freedom for me, and that holds great value. I spent endless hours considering my business and career, and I began applying for jobs. This was a humbling experience for me as a business advisor. As the pandemic extended into 2021, I had growing feelings of frustration, sadness, despair, and extreme uncertainty, and I was experiencing a lack of connection, respect, and trust in my marriage. Despite the pandemic situation turning around for the better in 2022, it felt like my life was falling apart. In many ways it was. The relationship breakdown in my marriage stirred up feelings of abandonment, loneliness, and rejection. I decided I needed to remember who I am, and the life I wanted to create. I invested in a life coaching program that became a transformational spiritual and personal growth experience. I gained clarity about how I was holding myself back, and the value of surrendering and letting go of what does not serve me. I learned to accept and trust myself, and to align my outlook and actions with my soul, heart, mind, energy, and body. Developing my self-awareness and embracing my strengths became my pathway to stability and a newfound presence to experience daily, and move forward from. I hope you resonate with my three examples of how leaning into my strengths as an includer, activator, and maximizer helped me to overcome adversity. When I am faced with challenging life events, I remind myself to focus on my strengths to live to my full potential.

Strength #1 – Includer

Including others is the only way I know that works for me and is how I have always lived my life. I am an instinctively accepting person and each day I think about stretching the circle wider. I want people to feel the warmth of the group, however, they choose to identify. Reflecting on my earliest memories, I am reminded of my love for meeting new people and making friends who are both like and unlike me. It breaks my heart to experience and observe injustice and inequality in the world. My brothers Keith and Douglas were Indigenous, and they felt the demoralizing effects of racism from students, as well as adults. My discomfort with social injustice has led me to take action. I chose a career where I could honor, recognize, and celebrate diversity, equity, and inclusion. Facilitating connections, making others feel included, as well as spreading positivity are very rewarding. I currently work as an Export Advisor, and my role is dedicated to helping Indigenous entrepreneurs across British Columbia grow their businesses into new markets. I feel comfortable engaging with, communicating, and listening to others. I often receive feedback that people feel understood and accepted by me. When I lead diversity and inclusion efforts, I am aligned with my values and honor my self-care and self-love.

Strength #2 – Activator

My strength as an activator means I am drawn to making things happen. The recurring question in my life is, "When can we start?" During the pandemic in early 2022, I was contacted by an entrepreneurship coach from Toronto, Canada via LinkedIn. He invited me to embark on a discovery process to learn about business ownership opportunities. After several months, I considered and evaluated the merits of several different business opportunities. I officially began operations of a franchise called Prep Academy Tutors in August 2022 with my business partner, Rhona Stanislaus. Our business is fully aligned with my values; I wake up every day excited to attract more clients and serve more families. Our certified teachers and tutors set us apart from other private tutoring companies and make us a reliable source for personalized education. Leaning into my strengths and taking the initiative to invest in a new business is self-love. It requires significant confidence and self-trust to take responsibility for the life I want to create.

Strength #3 – Maximizer:

My third strength is my foremost superpower as a maximizer. By nature, I am very persistent and determined. I am fascinated by strengths and happiest when I regularly celebrate my team and individual accomplishments. I spend a lot of time contemplating strengths in myself, in others, in partnerships, teams, organizations, associations, communities, countries, and the list goes on. I am drawn to uncovering strengths, and once I find a strength, I am compelled to nurture it, refine it, and stretch it toward excellence. Generally, I choose to spend time with people who appreciate my strengths, and I am attracted to others who know and cultivate their strengths. I believe we should all focus on our gifts and not what we lack. It is significantly more fun and productive in my lived experiences. A great source of pride for me is my role as co-founder of Northern Youth Leadership (NYL), alongside my dear friend and visionary, Kirsten Carthew. NYL brings together youth from across the Northwest Territories for remote land-based programming. NYL programming facilitates the development of leadership skills, life skills, and emotional resilience, and helps youth develop the inner and outer resources needed to overcome challenges, reach their full potential, and create positive change in their communities.

With all of my life experiences, the good, bad, and ugly, comes gratitude. When I was dealing with loss and grieving, it felt like an emotional crisis and non-love. I learned to respond with compassion, forgiveness, and optimism. I learned to trust myself, surround myself with my tribe, and do things that bring me joy. This helped me to get unstuck, and not get caught in a cycle of pain and heartache. I am grateful for my ability to look at my life situation with a spirit of positivity, energy, and enthusiasm. We all have choices, and sometimes our choices demand incredible strength and resiliency. When life is uncomfortable, sad, and confusing there's an opportunity to re-center and get into alignment. My self-love journey requires ongoing contemplation, acceptance, devotion, growth, and expansion. Self-love for me is knowing my strengths, trusting myself, standing firmly by my boundaries, and reclaiming my personal power to be a confident role model for my daughters. I am grateful for my parents who have always shown me the way of unconditional love and have always believed in me. I have immense admiration for my daughters who show love to me daily and continue to teach me more about love than they will ever know.

A quote that I've always found inspiring:

"Risk more than others think is safe. Care more than others think is wise. Dream more than others think is practical. Expect more than others think is possible."— Claude Thomas Bissell

Lessons Learned:

1. We all have unique gifts and strengths we can activate to achieve our highest potential. Aligning with your strengths should feel very natural and easy.
2. You have the power to transform your life, flow in the direction of your dreams, and manifest fulfillment, healthy relationships, and abundance.
3. Self-love is standing firmly by your boundaries, trusting yourself to live up to your full potential, and being a confident role model.

Mindset Tips:

1. I know my strengths and trust myself.
2. I am the powerful creator of my reality. I know what I want, and I choose it… daily.
3. I take radical responsibility for my results.

Aha Moments and Self-Reflections

Note your Thoughts

Yassminne Atallah

Yassminne Atallah is a soul of love living the human experience with a mission to inspire and help humans awaken to infinite love within to live a purposeful and authentic life. Her purpose is to be a living example, guide, teacher, mentor, healer, and coach!

Her inner knowing is a result of a spiritual initiation sparked through her journey of perseverance in banking, which lasted over 10 years until… it's for you to discover in the chapter!

Her biggest learning was that love, mainly self-love, is the key to her evolution and change as it empowered her to choose to live from her heart!

In a journey that is ever unfolding, and after mastering various methods in the field of self-development and spiritual evolution, Yassminne continues to learn and offer services to humans who are willing to love themselves enough to choose their own evolution and growth!

Connect with Yassminne:

https://instagram.com/yassinfinitelove/
https://www.facebook.com/YassInfiniteLove/
https://www.linkedin.com/in/yassminneatallah/

Chapter 17

Journey to Infinite Love

By Yassminne Atallah

Just like many kids out there, I had dreams since I was five years old—dreams of being an entrepreneur as I was born into a family that included a self-made man, my late grandfather, Fayez, may his soul rest in eternal peace. My dream was always about having my own company; something created for myself and my future. Obviously at the age of five, I did not really have the complete clarity of the business idea, yet I knew deep down, in my heart, that I will have my own business one day. I even mentioned it in my high school yearbook next to my graduation photo that I aspire to be a businesswoman.

Like many other kids, life generally surprises us and takes us on different journeys. Some of the journeys lead directly to our dream, as simple as a straight path, and other journeys go in different directions, a multifaceted path that eventually leads to the ultimate dream.

My journey went in a different direction until…

You will get to know as you read through!

Let me tell you a bit about me. I was born to a humble family from Aindara, a village located in Mount Lebanon. My late grandfather did not really have access to so much wealth in terms of money, but he had a wealth of values ranging from integrity, honesty, loyalty, perseverance, and much more. He did whatever he could to create a legacy for our family, which was a company that created a sustainable living for generations to follow. He left Lebanon and seized opportunities in the gulf region until he landed in the United Arab Emirates (UAE), where I was born. I consider myself blessed and proud to be part of the family and his lineage. His son, Mithkal, who is my father, decided not to join him initially in the company and rather have a career within the banking industry. My father's curiosity, enthusiasm, and eagerness to learn, understand and grow enabled him to land a job in one of the international banks in the UAE. After some time, my dad realized that instead of being just an employee at the bank, he could have a greater impact by joining his father's company alongside his two brothers. This ended up being the best decision, as this company to date has catered financially to at least four households covering the grandchildren's education, families' housing, and much more. Thank you, Grandpa and Baba!

A Journey from Lack to Prosperity and Growth

In our culture, like most Arab and Middle Eastern cultures, men are considered the bread earners, and women are perceived successful as housewives. Men's honor is directly linked to women in society, and therefore, primarily as means of protection of women and their reputation, women were not really given the space to blossom in business or to even work as employees. By the time I was born into this world in 1988, somehow this culture started to slightly change, especially with many members of the extended family, including my family, who travelled abroad and became exposed to different nationalities and cultures. This exposure helped them explore different mindsets, perspectives, and ways of living. Despite that, it was still a challenge to have women really step up, learn, and grow. Women's independence has been feared and judged by the society and culture. It was perceived as too much freedom and carried consequences, such as women stepping out of line with the norm and starting to make decisions or even changing the culture. The intrinsic impact and influence of women in society and culture was deeply understood, yet indirectly independence was not favored. I consider myself really lucky, as my mother, Randa, who was married to my father at the age of eighteen without completing her high school diploma, really strived to have me and my siblings complete our education. She lived in a city in the south of Lebanon, Sidon, and her family, precisely her late mother, Dalal, was completely pro education. They considered education for women to eventually secure a job in suitable industries, mainly schools and universities. This was work that secured an income, kept women safe, and balanced in their approach to life so they could cater for the household and their children's needs. Despite her background and the culture that she was married into, she managed to clear the path for my education because she knew how important it was in this day and age! Thank you, Mama!

A Journey from Women as Housewives to Women with Independence, Education and Work

I felt a great deal of responsibility being the eldest grandchild from the eldest son to my late grandfather I believed that I needed to make them all proud. This belief shaped my core reality and paved my educational and corporate journey.

My first milestone was achieved when I graduated from high school, Al Mawakeb School, at the age of sixteen. I was proudly one of the youngest ladies in my batch. Like the majority of parents in the region, and since they perceived me to be considerably young, their protection kept me from having the option of pursuing my bachelor's degree outside of the UAE, and Lebanon was not really an option since it constantly had political unrest and economic distress. Therefore, I was limited to choosing from the universities within UAE, and that also limited my options in terms of majors. Somehow, I was advised to be a pharmacist or a histopathologist, but these majors were offered in women-only universities, and coming from a school which had separate classes for girls and boys, I wanted to have the real-world experience. I then decided to join the American University in Dubai, where I completed my bachelor's degree in Business Administration with a major in Finance. I chose finance because I enjoyed numbers and math. Given that I have always been the youngest in class, I felt the need to match up with people all the time. It is like I felt the need to always be the best at what I did; like I am playing catch up all the time and this has led me to be impatient and highly competitive. I started university at the age of sixteen, I chose to excel and persevere, and decided to complete the four-years journey in three and half years instead by the age of nineteen. I completed university in December 2007, then decided to take some time off and enjoy a good three-months summer break in my village before I embarked on my working journey. It was honestly the best decision I have made, as it helped me really transition into the working world.

I had the option to choose to either work for the family business or anywhere else in the field, but take a wild guess of where I landed.

Holding the responsibility to be educated and the need to make my family proud led me to choose the banking sector. Initially, I worked in a local bank, then I moved into an international bank. Making that choice kind of upset my father, however, something within propelled me towards that direction, like my instincts or gut feeling. I just felt my path was different than that of the family's. I viewed life differently on all levels and I chose to pave my own way. As a child of the family, I am the sum of all the beliefs, conditioning, and values of the lineage and my own. I believe there is an inner knowing within each one of us and that leads us to either accept the existing composition of who we are, or change it gradually based on our life circumstances. Through my journey of self-discovery, I learned that in every step you assess what serves you in the current situation, and make decisions based on your future projection and where you aspire to be. If something is not aligned, you always have a choice to change it, like my choice to move away from the family business, which I will later share how well it served me.

I learned so much during my banking journey; the local bank was like a school for me. I soaked up all the knowledge like a sponge because it was the start of my career, and I was enthusiastic, optimistic, and ambitious. I grew within the bank despite challenges, though not at the pace that I expected and that resulted in me being unmotivated. Challenges were again based on perceptions that women do not deliver on the job as men do, and that typically they will end up being housewives—that's their destination! I learned, achieved, and grew, however, a feeling inside never left me. It was like I was never fulfilled. It felt like I was meant to do something different; that I was not in the right place, nor doing the right thing for me. Something was missing! Don't get me wrong here—the bank was great, the ambiance was great, the people there were like family, and I had meaningful friendships—but the Yassminne in me was missing in that place. It was a feeling that I really did not understand. I really did not know what to do or where to go next, but the next best possible step was to search for a job in another bank... that was the natural flow, and that's what happened! I decided to create a LinkedIn page, and within a week I was contacted by a headhunter who told me that there was an international bank recruiting and that I was a fit for the role. This news lit a spark in me! It was a new adventure, hence a renewed sense of enthusiasm and eagerness. I was amazed that this opportunity transpired so quickly and felt that it was meant to be! After finalizing my contract with the international bank, I submitted my resignation and faced different reactions from people; some cheered for my choice of stepping out of my comfort zone, while others said that I would fail since the culture would be different. I won't deny some of the comments took me off-guard and made me have some doubts alongside my excitement.

A Journey of Expansion from Local to International

I joined the international bank and felt like a goldfish in a tank of sharks with all kinds of other fish. By the time I joined the international bank, I had completed my master's degree in international finance from the American University in Dubai. Despite my five years of experience in banking and my higher university degree, I felt small and inexperienced. People at the bank spoke a language that I did not speak—banking jargon and business terminology which I wasn't as familiar with. There was a culture clash, moving from a friendly environment into a giant organization that was multicultural and involved different layers of authority with completely different systems and procedures. It took me time to adjust and understand how the bank and the people operated. Notwithstanding all of that, I remained being enthusiastic and eager to grow. I felt that there was room to evolve on that journey since they were advocating gender equality and inclusion. What I did not foresee was the fact that such organizations undergo multiple restructures during the years, and have the tendency to lay off people, demise departments, cancel positions, and downgrade employees. My expectations for growth were not met. I had to apply for my own promotion, which did not make any sense to me, and I had to find my way through, upward and forward. I felt unrecognized and to top it off, I received a review on my performance that mentioned I act immaturely, despite successfully completing all tasks at hand. In that moment, I had a choice; in order to grow and be recognized, I had to fit in, but this meant that I had to change myself and the way I do things. I did not realize it then that this meant going against my own authenticity—I felt like I lost my spark! Once again, the Yassminne in me went missing.

A new opportunity came my way when the bank decided to undergo a positive restructuring, and I was excited because I was joining a department that I always aspired to be part of. Despite all assurances that we would be safe, a week after receiving a letter of confirmation in that new department, we were told that we had three months left to search for another job within or outside the bank. I felt disappointed, yet I surrendered to this turn of events and decided not to look for a job, neither within nor outside the bank. I felt like this was a chance for me to pursue something different. I did not know what that was, but I just felt that perhaps this was my fate and I just needed to accept it! The bank was being very discrete about the announcement and no one was allowed to talk about it… that is until the heads of the previous department I worked for learned about the situation and decided to take me back with a promotion. While I felt grateful for this opportunity, I still experienced the same feelings I had before: I just felt unfulfilled, and that something was still missing. It was very confusing to me.

Thank you, leaders for that opportunity!

A Journey of Second Chances

I believe that my heart has led me on a journey, primarily to anchor the reality of the corporate journey, and to have an initiation into my spiritual journey—which I am forever grateful for. During that phase of unfulfillment and confusion, while I was absorbed by the previous department, I met a mentor who was already established in the world of coaching, mentoring, and spirituality. I chose to take multiple sessions with her to discover the root causes of my feelings and to unravel my purpose and passion in life. In one of the sessions, I remember her asking me about what I really wanted to do. She asked me repeatedly until I said that I love to help people. My mentor provided me with clarity and guidance so my journey could unfold. After my discussion with her, I realized that I was helping others all along, because one of my personal goals at work was to make at least one person smile a day!

I've always had the ability to read people and understand them, even before I decided to get a certificate in psychic readings and clairvoyance. People confided in me, trusted me, and sought advice, help and support. I just did not know before that there was a field that teaches how to become a professional in helping people. I started taking courses while I was still employed, which was helpful because I needed the funding for the courses. I learned Tarot Card Reading, Life Coaching, Hypnotherapy, Time Line Therapy, Reiki Energy Healing, Emotional Freedom Technique, and Quantum Healing. I was, and still am, very passionate about self-development, so as I was learning, I also took sessions with many spiritual mentors, teachers, and coaches; at least 100 sessions, if not more. I felt inspired, capable, and I had a vision of what I aspire to be now. I felt like there was a world outside of what I already knew!

A Journey from Unfulfillment and Confusion to Hope

Amidst the joy of finding hope and wanting to move in the direction of helping others, it was really challenging for me to leave the banking journey. It secured a steady income for me with the promise of a promotion, and a sound network. I felt really invested, and like a cargo ship that could not be redirected. My family, including my brother, Tamer, and sister, Ghina, witnessed my whole journey, and because they understood me, they really supported any decision I was going to make, which was a great relief. It felt like I was free from the responsibility of making them proud. I then realized that if I decided to leave comfortably without creating a shock to my system or way of life, I needed to prepare for that decision. The decision was kind of already made up in my mind, but the action took time until I secured the resources which would allow me to still fulfill my dreams when I left. And that's what happened.

For almost a year, I saved as much as I could, cut down on my expenses, and slightly adjusted my lifestyle to a way that I could maintain even if I didn't secure an income from this new profession right away. I got my promotion, and went for a short trip to Mauritius, my favorite country in the world, just to unwind. I used the trip as an opportunity to think deeply about my options and to decide whether to revisit my decision around staying or leaving. After deep contemplation on the trip, and upon my return, I asked for a sign. One morning as I walked into the bank with my phone in my hand, the first message that appeared on my phone was from Facebook and it said, "Stop searching for love in the same place where you once lost it." In that moment, I just knew that the path is clear and it's time to take action, so I resigned. It was a remarkable experience! From the moment I pressed the send button, I felt like I was unplugged from the matrix of the corporate world. I felt like my breath had changed, like I could really breathe, and I felt completely showered with hope. More importantly, I felt blessed to be able to take this opportunity and renew my life!

A Journey from the Known to the Unknown

I allowed my body and my mind to purge after quitting my job, and to catch up and align with my new reality. Meanwhile, I kept feeding my soul and evolving by learning other self-development tools, which would broaden my expertise and knowledge on the subject matter. I learned Self-Love Coaching using a special method called *I Love You, Me,* Sound Therapy using Crystal Singing Bowls, Psychic and Clairvoyant Readings and Healing, and I became a Reiki Master—and currently learning and mastering Womb Awakening and Healing. Even though I ventured into the unknown, I had some plans in place. We all know one thing that is absolutely true—plans don't always turn out the way we want them to! This was a blessing in disguise that motivated me to establish my company, which includes coaching services and crystal (semi-precious stones) products, two areas that complement each other. I found myself finally fulfilling a dream of being an entrepreneur—a businesswoman! Though the business idea was there, the name had not been decided. I had a vision of my logo when I began this journey. So, in one of our sibling meetings, we brainstormed and aligned the logo with potential names. We landed on *Infinite Love*. Today, I am the owner and founder of *Infinite Love,* which offers a range of coaching, healing, and facilitation services, alongside a range of semi-precious stones. The name says it all; this has been my journey to Infinite Love!

It has been almost four years since I left my corporate journey, and these are some lessons I've learned thus far:

- Love is all we need: After leaving the bank, I realized that I chose to follow in my father's footsteps in order to be recognized by him. Subconsciously, I decided that if I were like him, and I continued his journey in banking and succeeded, he would be happy and proud of me. Without total awareness, the responsibility I took directed my life choices, so this choice was not made from a space of self-love. Hence the resistance, yet the silver lining was my spiritual initiation.
- All paths eventually lead to the same destination: You don't need to beat yourself up for any decision you make or for taking a longer route—never regret any decision. You never know which path has the most to learn from, which will help you grow and be ready for what is to come next. What is meant for you will never pass you by… this is so true! I didn't think that my journey in banking would be a spiritual initiation that led me into creating my own business.
- Plan and take your time; there is no need to rush: Even when you plan, it doesn't mean that plans will go as you

hoped. It is important to venture into the unknown with agility, adaptability, resilience, and courage. I had accounted for certain expenses in life but I hadn't budgeted for a business. I still executed because I believed I needed to anchor my calling and my dream. Always follow your heart!

Alongside the learnings, these are some mindset tips which would help you in persevering and moving forward:

- Life is in constant change: This is something we need to accept to be able to surrender and be in flow. Otherwise, we create unnecessary resistance which results in undesired experiences, feelings, emotions, and a closed mindset. When you surrender, you give yourself space to digest situations better, and remain resourceful in finding solutions and creative ways to lead your life. Obstacles are opportunities that help you learn and grow. When you make that choice, you start seeing life as an experience that is happening ***for*** you instead of ***to*** you!
- Value yourself regardless of people's recognition: I was met with comments about how I would not succeed in an international bank, how I was immature in the way I behaved, how I was too young for a promotion, how I couldn't handle that many responsibilities, and much more. I always put people on a pedestal and undermined my knowledge and experience, my value, and my worth. I trusted people and their experiences more than I trusted and valued myself. This made my foundations shaky due to low self-confidence and self-esteem, which held me back in many situations, like making decisions for myself. I stopped believing fully in myself and I had to build that back up when I left. In unknown territory, you get to be in control of your life, leading your way through because if you are a lone wolf like me, no one will come and tell you that you did a great job. You have to honor yourself! So why wait?

Make the choice to honor yourself every moment! Your life is meaningful regardless of any possible perceptions! If you don't exist, the life you are living doesn't not exist. So, believe in yourself and value who you are!

- Never give up or be disheartened by rejections, delays, no income, or no outcome! Follow your dream and build your worth and faith! You never know when one day an opportunity might knock on your door, and suddenly you have an empire, you are creating a legacy, or you are famous and shining like a STAR!

That's just a sneak peek into an aspect of my journey of self-discovery, which continues to be enlightening, fulfilling, and expansive. It's the journey that helped me expand my awareness, and strengthened my self-love so I can be empowered enough to make decisions purely from my heart instead of decisions based on my surroundings or my past.

So, would you be willing to love yourself enough to embark on that journey and follow your heart?

Lessons Learned:

1. Love is all we need. There is always a silver lining.
2. All paths eventually lead to the same destination.
3. Plan and take your time; there is no need to rush. Always follow your heart!

Mindset Tips:

1. Accept that life is in constant change; life is an experience that is happening for you instead of to you!
2. Value yourself regardless of people's recognition.
3. Never give up!

Aha Moments and Self-Reflections

Note your Thoughts

Conclusion

Your journey with us has come to an end… for now.

We hope that you have discovered that we all can learn to love ourselves. *Self Love Elevated* is a timeless piece. You can be five or seventy-five years of age and still learn about self-worth, self-love, and self-acceptance.

I hope that what you have read between these pages has been insightful and helped guide you to understand more about the process of self-love and how important it is. It is a journey of love, kindness, and understanding of self. It is a personal journey, not a "one size fits all" description. It is about finding out what's working and not working for you. It is about being real with yourself and asking yourself some very pointed questions. It involves reworking schedules and digging into your heart and soul to ignite the fire that gets you out of bed in the morning. It's about looking at yourself in the mirror and knowing you are worthy and deserving of the life you want. It's about being open to receiving that life.

Open yourself up to the knowledge that there is a different path. It's about choice and understanding that although there may be obstacles in your path, there will also be unlimited opportunities. Self-discovery and self-love are a way of life, not a destination.

There will be highs and lows but recognizing your love for yourself is the most important commodity you can have.

Our wish, as authors, is to inspire you to dig deep. Find your passion and purpose and have a love affair with yourself. The world is waiting for you. The path may not be easy, but I have learned that one of the best questions to ask is, "What am I to learn from this experience?"

The lessons you learn along the way will be part of the journey to self-love.

The stories shared with you are raw and vulnerable, from the heart and soul of each author. With each chapter, we hope you learned new lessons and mindset tips that will allow you to reflect on your life through journaling in the note pages.

A strong sense of self-worth and knowing what fuels you are the foundation for a successful life and business. You must feel worthy and ready to receive all the blessings you deserve. It took me several thousands of dollars to figure out what I already knew deep within myself.

Self-love elevated is the higher essence of everything good in your life. The world is shifting; women want the flexibility of working from home. This means more freedom, fun, and family stability. This is a paradigm shift and a movement to a new space. It is knowing peace and solitude, holding boundaries for your mental health, and knowing that you matter. You aren't alone.

We are all connected with communities wanting collaboration and calling to pay it forward. It is said that when each of us shines our light, it gives permission for others to shine theirs.

This is your time.

Join us at our Get You Visible Community

Do You Dream of Being a Published Author?

The best part of what I do is bring people together to write, share, and inspire those who may feel alone or need healing. Your story could help to heal others.

My team will guide you through the writing process so your idea can become a reality to be shared on worldwide distribution channels.

A book has been referenced as an authority piece for centuries and is known to be one of the best ways to gain instant credibility and visibility with clients in the online and offline space.

Let's talk if you have a story to share and want to become a published author or co-author in a collaborative. Book your complimentary call with me.

https://getyouvisible.as.me/Discovery-Call-With-Heather

Here's to your story and someone waiting to read it.

Heather Andrews

https://getyouvisible.com

Get You Visible is home to over 200 published, 40 books published and 28 #1 Amazon Best-Sellers — Let us help you!

Manufactured by Amazon.ca
Bolton, ON

33382974R00142